THE DOUBLE HELIX OF EDUCATION AND THE ECONOMY

Sue E. Berryman
Thomas R. Bailey

Institute on Education and the Economy
Teachers College/Columbia University

ISBN 1-882217-00-4

TABLE OF CONTENTS

ACKNOWLEDGEMENTS

We acknowledge our debt to our colleagues, three of them in particular: Jacob Mincer, whose seminal research on human capital and the dynamics of labor markets framed our understanding of the relationship between education, training, and economic outcomes; Sylvia Scribner—whose work was unfortunately cut short by her death in 1991—who had begun to chart the major questions that the field needs to confront about the nature of workplace cognitive functioning and learning; and P. Michael Timpane, who backed and supported our work, and, in the early 1980s, intuited changes in the economy that would force a fundamental rethinking of our educational system.

Our thinking about this subject has also been illuminated by the contributions of Joseph Altonji, Ann Bartel, Charles Benson, Tora Bikson, John Black, David Bloom, Susan Boardman, Erwin Flaxman, Thomas Glennan, Charles Harrington, Yoshio Higuchi, Gareth Hoachlander, Joseph Kett, Frank Lichtenberg, Victoria Marsick, Laura Martin, Lorraine McDonnell, Gary Natriello, Thierry Noyelle, Senta Raizen, Lauren Resnick, Patricia Sachs, Nachum Sicherman, Seymour Spilerman, Cathleen Stasz, Joy Stevens, Hong Tan, Roger Vaughan, Maris Vinovskis, and Harold Watts.

We also warmly acknowledge the support of many research centers and foundations. Much of the research that undergirds this book was made possible by the sustained support of the Office of Educational Research and Improvement (OERI) of the U.S. Department of Education. The research also had the generous support of the National Council for Vocational Education, the National Assessment of Vocational Education, the U.S. Department of Labor, and Teachers College, Columbia University.

A conference sponsored by the Institute on Education and the Economy where many of the ideas in this book were explored was supported by the Carnegie Corporation, The National Center for Research in Vocational Education, the American Express Company, the Edna McConnell Clark Foundation, the Joyce Foundation, Frederick Schultz, and the Howard Heinz Endowment. The Carnegie Corporation also supported the writing and publication of this book.

We have, in addition, benefitted greatly by our partnerships with The RAND Corporation, the National Center for Research in Vocational Education, and the Eisenhower Center for the Conservation of Human Resources.

We are deeply grateful to the Spencer Foundation, which provided the seed money, the long-term investment, and the encouragement to challenge and rethink the premises of human capital research and policy in this country. The Spencer Foundation, by stimulating people to talk to each other about the issues of education and the American economy, created the context for the research and policy analysis that followed, and ultimately made this book possible.

Our work and our thinking has also been guided by members of our national advisory board: Rex Adams, Michael Bailin, William Birenbaum, Anthony Carnevale, Barbara Christen, Dennis de Tray, Eleanor Farrar, Badi Foster, Sol Hurwitz, Stanley Lebergott, Marsha Levine, William Mauritz, Daniel Morley, Robert Reischauer, Rodney Riffel, Peter Rossi, and Isabel Sawhill.

We thank Morton Inger, who read and critiqued many drafts of this book, Eric Larsen, for his careful editing, and Joseph Meyers, who diligently processed all of our words.

1

INTRODUCTION

BACKGROUND

The thinking and some of the research on which this book is based began in 1985. At that time the Institute on Education and the Economy began to challenge and rethink the premises that governed much of the accepted thinking and policy about relationships between the U.S. economy and our educational system.

This book is about economic activity and learning. We found that how the United States organizes its education—what we teach, to whom, when, but especially how—approximately matches how the country had organized economic activity for decades. However, we found economic activity changing, although hardly in all industries or in all companies. These changes were gradually rendering education as traditionally delivered more and more out of step with what its graduates needed to know and who needed to know it.

At the same time, a powerful research base, cognitive science, revealed that schooling, especially its pedagogy, was poorly organized for learning, whatever the economic environment in which individuals had to deploy what they knew. What was startling was that the two strands came together. The skill requirements of restructured workplaces and optimal ways of organizing learning fit one another.

The voyage which culminated in this book did not represent a resumption of the 1970s concerns about youth unemployment. Some sophisticated analyses and program experiments were conducted during that period. However, we felt that this work had been done without an adequate understanding of the sources of youth unemployment. The employment difficulties that many youth experienced during this period reflected not just labor over-supply as the result of the baby boom, but also deeper shifts in demand that were murky and could not have been well appreciat-ed at that time. Thus, the nation's image of the problem at that time was inevitably partial, producing policies that were capable, at best, of only pallid success. Some years later *The Forgotten Half* documented the long-term decline in the wages of high school dropouts and graduates, a decline that continued even as the youth over-supply problem eased and that reflected the inade-quacy of our earlier problem definition.

Nor were our concerns prompted by *A Nation At Risk* and similar reports. In general, these reports argued that the United States had had a good school system subsequently compromised by an emphasis on access and "relevance." They associated the U.S. economic decline with the deterioration in the quality of education, identifying higher standards and stiffer academic requirements (the "new basics") as the solution. We sensed that these reports had seriously misdiagnosed the problem and that the new basics would not solve it.

We focused on two features of the landscape. They were not features that others would have automatically put together, coming as they did out of completely different research traditions. This book is about the nature, confluence, and policy implications of these two features.

One was the human capital implications of a restructuring U.S. economy. The mid-1980s was a time of acrimonious debate about trends in the skill requirements of the economy. The prevailing view was that, overall, the economy was "downskilling" rather than "upskilling." However, research then being conducted at Columbia University and at a few other places on restructuring industries suggested not that the prevailing view was wrong, but that the research on which it was based had caught the endgame of the mass production era in the U.S. economy. Under a mass production regime, even flexible technologies such as computers are used in the ways that technologies had traditionally been used—to minimize worker discretion.

However, the Columbia University and other research was beginning to pick up a shift in American manufacturing and service industries from mass to flexible production, a shift accompanied by fundamental changes in the organization of work and in the skills required of workers at all levels in the organization. Wherever these changes occurred, they ended up reducing the number of low-skill jobs, restructuring some share of low-skill jobs to require higher-level skills, and changing what workers needed to know, how they needed to use their knowledge, and the long-term value of any current stock of knowledge and skill.

The other feature of the landscape on which we focused was learning. One reason for concentrating on learning was our sense of the long-term direction of the U.S. economy. If we were right about the direction, we foresaw a profound challenge to our educational and training system. Although we saw the implications in only dim outline, we anticipated that these would involve changing what our people learned, who learned it, how they learned it, and when they learned it.

- Ultimately, the system would have to find some way to extend serious, coherent education to the non-baccalaureate-bound and to the less-educated members of our experienced labor force. Our schools took seriously the learning of the baccalaureate-bound, but the rest were being less prepared than carried along. However, what was happening to the wages for less-skilled work suggested that schools had to position all of their students for middle- and higher-skill jobs. Similarly, employers invested training in the better-educated and in those in the high-skill occupations (Tan, 1989; Vaughan & Berryman, 1989), but not in the less-educated. What was happening to the job responsibilities of even shop floor workers in restructuring workplaces implied the need for employers to train employees at all levels in the organization.

- Schools would have to reconceive their task as positioning their students for subsequent years of learning. The reality of the emerging economy was change. Individuals needed the ability to create options for themselves and to be flexible and adaptable. Whether older or younger, they needed an educational underpinning that would let them continue to learn.

- The skill distinctions between higher- and lower-skill jobs were blurring. This reality did not fit the schools' traditional organization into academic versus vocational curricula.

- Early returns on restructuring workplaces indicated that the contexts for deploying knowledge and skill had shifted dramatically. We sensed, again in only vague outline, that these new work contexts and the traditional school contexts for learning were profoundly out of step with each other.

A second reason that we focused on learning was that we saw a building indictment of traditionally organized learning. This indictment was coming out of a powerful research base, cognitive science.[1] This research looked to be a slash across the canvas for schooling and training of all kinds—whether elementary and secondary education, college, professional schools, adult literacy programs, military training, or corporate training. No less than changes in the economy, this research also constituted a challenge to how we structured learning.

At the heart of this research was the presumption that intelligence and expertise are built out of interaction with the environment, not in isolation from it. It thus challenged our traditional distinctions between

- head and hand
- academic and vocational education
- knowing and doing
- abstract and applied
- education and training
- school-based and work-based learning

This research took on a range of questions germane to relationships between education and the economy (Raizen, 1989). What is known about the differences between effective performance and less-skilled performance, and how do individuals acquire expertise in a job? What are the relationships between what are usually considered basic or general skills (literacy, numeracy, reasoning skills, ability to solve problems), knowledge

---

[1]Cognitive science is an interdisciplinary field that encompasses psychologists, linguists, anthropologists, computer scientists, philosophers, and neuroscientists. The word "cognitive" refers to perceiving and knowing, and cognitive science is the science of mind. Cognitive scientists seek to understand perceiving, thinking, remembering, understanding language, learning, and other mental phenomena. Their research is quite diverse, ranging from observing children learning mathematics or experienced workers handling the cognitive demands of their jobs through programming computers to do complex problem solving or analyzing the nature of meaning (Stillings et al., 1987).

in a specific domain, and competency in a related job or profession? How do people actually solve problems on the job, and what are the skills and competencies that characterize good work performance? How effectively do people transfer their formal school-based instruction to situations outside school and apply it on the job? What is the role of apprenticeship, and what are its modern equivalents?

The implications of this work were being used primarily to critique elementary and secondary education. However, we sensed that the nation's educational and training systems did not differ, particularly in their pedagogic strategies, whatever the rhetoric about their differences. All of these systems seemed to have very limited success because they had similar pedagogic problems. Americans share the common experience of elementary and secondary schooling. This shared experience frames our ideas and models of what learning environments should look like, whether called a college classroom, an adult literacy class, or a corporate training classroom. Thus, we surmised that the pedagogic problems of our elementary and secondary schools got reproduced even in training systems that were generally thought of as nontraditional, such as employer-sponsored training programs.

In sum, we looked at the nation's economic and educational problems through two lenses: the human capital implications of a restructuring U.S. economy and the implications of cognitive science for designing powerful learning environments. Educationally, we assumed that any meaningful reform of U.S. education had to start from and build on two realities:

- what people need to know and to know how to do in nonschool settings

- how they learn whatever they need to know most effectively and efficiently

In other words, the core issue was learning: what and how. We
saw the point of reform repeatedly lost, means becoming confused
with ends, and even central players often apparently forgetting the
central objective. However, all reforms, whether choice, teacher
retraining, assessment redesign, or whatever, matter only as they
produce significant improvements in learning that students need
for different dimensions of their lives.

In terms of the causal relationships between educational
reform and economic gains, we found ourselves at variance with
prevailing assumptions about the effect of improved skills on
economic competitiveness. During the 1980s it was assumed that
school change, interpreted as higher standards and stiffer academic
requirements, would improve skills, which in turn would improve
economic competitiveness.[2]

A Nation At Risk's equation of improved skills with improved
economic competitiveness was too simple. It did not reflect a
number of factors that affect an industry's competitiveness, of
which the skills of its labor force are only one. A far more critical
factor under the control of the firm is leadership and management,
as these play out in the firm's market strategy, production
processes and organization of work, time horizons, or investments
in physical and human capital.

Some years later other reports, such as *America's Choice: High
Skills or Low Wages!* (Commission on the Skills of the American
Workforce, 1990), started out with a more sophisticated argu-

---

[2]Obviously, national and individual competitiveness need to be kept separate.
Improved skills clearly increase *individuals'* competitiveness in the labor market.
We took issue only with the causal link between improved skills and *national*
economic competitiveness.

ment. These stated that high skills improve productivity and thus wages *only* if the employer has organized work to take advantage of those skills, an argument with which we agree. However, with minor exceptions, *America's Choice* proposed a solution that de facto fell back into the argument of *A Nation At Risk*: improve the education and training system to improve individuals' skills to shift the economy toward workplaces reorganized to make productive use of additional skill. This strategy increases the supply of skilled workers and constitutes a supply-side solution to the problem. The implicit chain of reasoning is that boosting the supply of higher-skilled workers will reduce the wages (price) of this labor and thus the cost of moving to an organization of work that depends more heavily on it. Thus, employers will have an incentive to shift from workplaces based on low skills to ones based on higher skills.

We took issue with the arguments of both *A Nation At Risk* and *America's Choice*. First, the evidence, laid out in chapter 2, was suggesting to us that although firms still face a choice between traditional and more innovative production systems, shifts in the economic context have changed the terms of that choice. These changes have created incentives, independent of the supply of educated and less-educated workers, for firms to reform the organization of their production processes. In this environment firms find it increasingly difficult and costly to hang on to their traditional approaches.

Second, by itself, strengthening education and thus the skills of its graduates will take years to begin to affect the behavior of firms. It is a solution akin to "pushing on a string." If firms are as committed to the traditional system as *America's Choice* implies, the gradual effects of an upgraded workforce will be swamped by policies such as the Free Trade Agreement with Mexico.

At the same time, we felt that if employers decided to pull on the string, that string should not be anchored in a low-skill labor force. Thus, given our reading of the long-term direction of the U.S. economy and our view that solid skills multiply *individuals'* economic options, we believed it incumbent on our policymakers and educators to focus on how to produce dramatic improvements in learning for all students, especially for the non-college-bound.

ARGUMENT AND ORGANIZATION OF THE BOOK

Chapter 2 synthesizes the Institute's and others' research on the skill and educational implications of a changing economy. It pulls together several separate strands of research: trends in the wage returns to education; changes in the employment share of those occupations that use a higher-than-average level of education; industry case studies; and changes in the educational profiles of those employed in industries undergoing technological innovation.

Using the lens of cognitive science, chapter 3 synthesizes the research record to reveal that our schools organize learning poorly, violating what we know about how people learn most effectively and the conditions under which they apply their knowledge appropriately to new situations. Chapter 4 delineates an alternative organization of learning that promises to make markedly more effective use of students' learning time and to involve the less motivated more deeply and productively in learning. A century of thought, research, and trials gives us the outline of what effective learning situations look like. They look very different from how most schools now organize learning. Chapter 5 develops three fundamental recommendations and shows the implications of these ideas for current educational reform discussions.

2

CHANGES IN THE WORKPLACE

INTRODUCTION

Profound changes have reshaped the nation's economy during the last twenty years. These changes have been driven by intensified international competition, a proliferation of products, accelerating product cycles, a faster pace of change in production technologies, and a generally heightened level of uncertainty. These developments have also altered the nature of work and the skills required for front-line workers, managers, and professionals. Employees need more formal education and a broader understanding of the context in which they work. They must also have the ability to operate more independently with less direct supervision.

In this chapter we first discuss the nature of the economic developments that are driving changes in skill and educational requirements. The educational implications of these changes can be understood in terms of two broad approaches to production and economic activity. After describing these two strategies, we argue that developments during the last decade are forcing employers to shift from one strategy to the other. In the subsequent section, we draw on case studies of the apparel, banking, and textile industries, carried out at Columbia University in the 1980s (Bailey, 1988, 1989; Bertrand & Noyelle, 1988), to present concrete examples of how the economic and market forces confronting firms have resulted in changes in production strategies and in the nature of work. We then present a variety of empirical evidence supporting the argument that skill and educational requirements are in fact rising. The last section discusses in more detail the types of skills that are increasingly in demand.

CAUSES OF THE CHANGING ECONOMY

Broad developments in the underlying economy and the nature of competition underlie the changes in the production strategies and the resulting shifts in skill and educational requirements that have occurred in the last twenty years. The most significant characteristics of these economic trends is that they have increased the extent and pace of change and the level of uncertainty.

Internationalization

Increased international competition is one of the most important influences pushing changes in production processes and work organization. The sum of all imports and exports was 12 percent of the total U.S. GNP in 1960 and 31 percent in 1989 (U.S. Department of Commerce, 1991, p. 431). Moreover, the concern of domestic producers is not simply that trade has increased, but rather that the balance of trade has shifted against the U.S. Yet, in and of itself, globalization would not necessarily lead to any particular changes in the nature of work. Indeed, in the 1970s U.S. producers sought to beat back international competition by introducing labor-saving technology accompanied by attempts to keep down wages and therefore skills. But internationalization has coincided with other changes in market conditions.

Proliferation of products and services

As a 1988 Office of Technology Assessment report puts it, "Many markets formerly dominated by a comparatively small number of relatively homogenous products are becoming 'boutique' markets, combining a wide range of specialties" (Office of Technology Assessment, 1988, p. 70). Studies of retailing show significant increases in "stock keeping units" (an indication of the number of products for sale) over the last decade (Stanback, 1990). Although there are still many opportunities to produce white underwear or corn flakes, these types of basic commodities account for a diminishing share of the market.

This development involves a shift from growth based primarily on increased sales of standardized goods and services to attempts to sell more varied and customized products. For example, through the mid-1970s, consumer banks focused their marketing efforts on bringing new clients into the banking system. In the 1960s, only 25 percent of households in the United States had checking and savings accounts, while by the early 1980s, almost 90 percent had such accounts. Rising household incomes not only created a demand for basic banking services but also increased the market for more specialized consumer financial instruments. Fifteen years ago consumer banks in the United States offered six basic products; today customers in the most progressive retail banks can choose from over 100 products.

Although fashion has always been important at the upper end of the apparel markets, during the last two decades changing styles have come to dominate much larger segments. Innovative designers and producers (initially most were foreign) saw potential markets for fashion-oriented products for middle-income consumers. In earlier decades, there were two fashion seasons. Now some designers change their lines six times a year, and retailers want to have almost continuous changes in their stock.

The greater segmentation of markets and the faster changing of styles have shrunk the market for large production runs of identical garments. Apparel industry analysts argue that commodity products such as men's underwear and socks that are sold all year account for only about 20 percent of the apparel market, and that this share is likely to fall. Moreover, even the most basic commodities now come in many more styles and colors than previously.

During the 1980s, most textile and apparel plants increased the number of styles and products that they were producing. In many cases, the number of styles was increased or the average production run was cut by a factor of ten. Even mills producing denim, which is the epitome of a standardized, basic commodity, have increased the number of styles produced at any one time from 2 or 3 to 30 or more (Bailey, 1988, 1989).

Accelerated product and process innovation

Like many industries, banking, textiles, and apparel enjoyed periods of stability during the 1950s, 1960s, and early 1970s but are now undergoing periods of frantic innovation and technological change. This environment of change, as much as the actual characteristics of the new technology, new products, or new trade patterns, often forces fundamental changes in firm strategies. Traditional approaches geared to a more stable environment no longer work.

For example, it takes only a few hours to process most apparel and other soft goods, yet it often takes up to a year between an order and the arrival of the goods on the retail shelves. As long as styles changed infrequently, this was not a serious problem. But as mass markets began to break up, and production needs became more difficult to predict, retailers found more frequently that they ran out of quick-selling items during the season (this is called a "stockout") and were stuck at the end of the season with large quantities of slower-selling goods that they were forced to mark down. Forced markdowns have increased by 50 percent during the last decade. Losses from stockouts amount to 8 percent of sales (Office of Technology Assessment, 1987). In 1984, the apparel and retail industries lost about $25 billion from stockouts, excessive markdowns, and excess inventories. This accounted for almost one quarter of the total retail value of all apparel sold in the United States that year (Harding, 1988).

One result of this growing uncertainty in an environment of intensified competition is that firms are placing increasing emphasis on reducing the time that it takes to develop, produce, and distribute a product. The development of just-in-time inventory systems has accelerated production cycles. Toyota was able to cut its domestic manufacturing, distribution, and sale cycle from four to six weeks in 1982 to only eight days in 1987 (Stalk, 1988).

While just-in-time systems shorten the production cycle, progressive firms have also tried to shorten the time it takes to develop new products. Much has been made of the ability of Japanese firms to develop projects with significantly shorter lead times than U.S. firms. One survey found that, in comparison with U.S. firms, Japanese automobile firms completed design projects in two-thirds the time with only one-third the engineering hours (Clark, Chew, & Fujimoto, 1987). Thus changing consumer markets, new computerized technologies, and emerging production techniques have accelerated production and product development. Firms that fail to take steps to develop more flexible and responsive strategies will be at an increasing disadvantage.

Similar strategies are now being implemented in the United States with great fanfare. Since the mid-1980s, as style changes in apparel and textiles have accelerated, leaders in those industries have turned from a virtual obsession with automation to an equally strong preoccupation with reducing production and delivery times, called "Quick Response" in the industry. Quick Response allows retailers to order with shorter lead times and to reorder hot items during the season. In some cases these efforts have cut lead times from several months to six to ten weeks.

TWO PRODUCTION STRATEGIES

The intensification of national and international competition, the proliferation of products, the faster pace of change, and the growing level of uncertainty have forced American businesses to look for new ways of organizing their production processes. These organizational changes in turn lead to shifts in the nature of work and the skill and educational needs of that work. In order to understand this transformation, two broad alternative approaches to production need to be considered.

U.S. business rose to power during the early and middle decades of the 20th century on the basis of a production system designed to drive down the unit cost of standardized products produced in large numbers. This traditional or "robust" production system

> emphasizes narrowly defined jobs that can be filled by interchangeable, low-skilled workers; large inventory buffers that minimize the disruption caused by production errors or poor quality parts; extra employees to cope with higher absenteeism; sophisticated quality control inspection systems and specialized personnel to catch defects after production is completed; and technologies designed to minimize the number of workers and to control or limit worker discretion (Thomas & Kochan, 1990, pp. 19-20).

This system had many advantages. It reduced unit costs and training needs and insulated the firm's production process from turnover and absenteeism. But while the system allowed firms to operate with lower-skilled workers, this benefit was bought at a cost. Technology had to be specially designed to minimize worker control and limit worker discretion. Front-line production workers were expected to handle only routine problems, requiring many supervisors, managers, and support personnel to deal with any change in procedures or unexpected difficulties. In effect, employers made a tradeoff between low skill levels and high levels of detailed planning, close supervision, and managerial effort.

The traditional system is most advantageous when products or services and production systems and technologies rarely change. When change is infrequent, the cost of developing the specialized equipment and processes required to routinize tasks can be recouped over the long period in which tasks do not change. A stable environment also minimizes the number of unexpected problems that low-skilled workers would not be able to handle.

During most of the postwar era, the advantages firms derived from being able to use a low-skilled work force outweighed the costs associated with using the traditional system. Standardization and mass production were the goals of both manufacturing and large service providers such as insurance companies and banks.

But recent economic developments, especially the acceleration of change, challenge the viability of the traditional system, which is so dependent on predictability. Flexibility, fast response time, and innovation, as much as cost, are now the keys to growth and competitiveness. Constant change requires that a particular production technology or process be put to many uses. As a result, there are many fewer opportunities for routinization. Managers can still keep down skills, but they will have to make a much larger investment in designing work aids and helping unskilled workers cope with a growing number of unpredictable problems.

Rather than the low-skill, high-control system characteristic of mass production, the new economic environment requires the integration of traditionally separate functional roles (design, engineering, marketing, manufacturing, and so forth), flatter organizational hierarchies, decentralization of responsibility, and greater employee involvement at all levels. While the traditional system has advantages in terms of control and reduced training and skill needs, the alternative system is more responsive and flexible and more conducive to continuous innovation. In effect, by making lower-level workers more flexible and skilled and by giving them more responsibility and discretion, their jobs incorporate some of the supervisory, planning, repair, maintenance, and support functions that were previously reserved for managers or specialists. This has the added advantage of saving time and eliciting positive participation from front-line workers in the development of new products and processes. This type of system is therefore based on much less direct supervision, but requires workers with higher skills.

THE CHANGING NATURE OF WORK: CONCRETE EXAMPLES

We now turn to some concrete examples of evolving workplaces in which changing markets and technology are reshaping the organization of production and altering skill requirements. These descriptions of changes in the nature of work are based on case studies of the banking, textile, and apparel industries carried out by the Institute on Education and the Economy at Teachers College, Columbia University.

Banking

Increasing computerization is leading to the elimination of a considerable amount of routine manual processing—the handling of printed forms, paper-based files, manual records, manual calculations, and similar tasks—that in the past supported the production of banking services. This transformation is affecting all workers, although its most direct impact is on low-level personnel (file clerks, messengers, statistical clerks, and similar personnel) by eliminating the tasks that they traditionally carried out and shifting their functions to middle-level personnel working with automated systems.

Middle-level personnel are also taking on a broader array of functions. Increasing computerization of banking products is bringing together information once scattered among various employees and departments. As a result, many middle-level jobs traditionally oriented towards "order taking"—filling out forms to initiate the clerical production process—increasingly involve "serving"—providing customers with the various pieces of information necessary to provide the customized mix of services that will best answer their needs. Therefore, many of the responsibilities associated with managing the interaction with customers are filtering down from upper-tier to middle-tier personnel. For example, a corporate account officer may now delegate much of the day-to-day interaction with corporate customers (money transfers, issuance of letters of credit, and so forth) to a subordinate corporate service representative. This type of shift is further complicated by the proliferation of banking services. During the 1980s, banks that had previously offered consumers primarily checking and savings accounts, expanded their services to include dozens of different types of accounts and credit instruments. One result is a shift toward finding better-educated middle-level workers who have a stronger capacity to comprehend both the bank's services and capabilities and the customer's needs. That means a shift away from lesser-educated clerks who worked primarily on specialized form-handling tasks.

Textiles

Similar developments are taking place in the textile industry. For example, in 1987, Swift Textiles, Inc., a subsidiary of the Canadian corporation Dominion Textile Incorporated, the largest denim manufacturer in the world, carried out a major modernization program in its Columbus, Georgia, plants. At the same time, the firm expanded the number of denim weaves and colors, stepped up efforts to monitor and anticipate market changes, and moved toward establishing a system of quick response.

One of the most dramatic changes caused by the upgrading program was an immediate need for dozens of fixers trained to repair and maintain the new equipment. The company found that some of the fixers they had already employed could not keep up with the training, and there was a shortage of other workers who were adequately prepared and who might be promoted to the maintenance jobs. Swift designed a pre-fixer training course to teach students to do such things as "accurately use a calculator for basic mathematical calculations; use basic mathematical formulae in order to calculate pressures, voltage, amperage, electrical resistance, and temperatures; determine acceptable tolerances of machine parts based on machine drawings; accurately read machine drawings and derive specific dimensions from them; and differentiate among discrete components in simple electrical schematic diagrams." This course consisted of 15 three-hour classes, and it is indicative of the skills problem faced by the firm that of the 32 students who entered the first class, only six successfully completed the course. Most of the students who failed to complete the course did not have an adequate background in math.

Traditionally, fixers did not need these types of skills. In the past, fixer training had been entirely informal. Interested workers were chosen to follow experienced hands around the plant until they were judged to be adequately prepared. Although the traditional looms and spinning machines had been intricate, they were based on mechanical principles that were usually familiar to young men through their experience with cars or farm machinery. One training manager put it simplistically though graphically, "In the old days all the mechanic had to do to fix a loom was to get a bigger hammer." But the operation of the newest looms could not be observed. Indeed, this is consistent with broader research on the educational effects of computerization: Observational (visually based) learning has been replaced by learning acquired primarily through symbols, whether verbal or mathematical. To fix the new machines, technicians had to be able to represent their structures symbolically in their heads. To do this, they also had to follow complicated manuals, diagrams, and updates provided by the machine manufacturers.

Faced with intensified international competition and increasingly demanding customers who wanted faster production and delivery, Swift began to incorporate some support functions such as machine maintenance, inventory control, and record keeping into the jobs of operators. For example, as managers stepped up efforts to speed throughput and to prevent downtime for the expensive, high-capacity looms, they worked out a system to record the causes of stoppages for each loom. The system depended on the ability of loom operators to diagnose the problem and to enter a code corresponding to that problem on the loom's electronic control panel. Thus not only must these operators be able to locate the codes on a multipage list, but they must be able to make some judgments about the causes of machine problems, not all of which are obvious. As one training manager said, "We are simply asking a lot more of these weavers than we used to."

Even the loom cleaners, who are among the lowest-paid workers in the plant, now must at least be able to read instructions and punch numbers into a keypad.

As a result of these developments, Swift has established an educational program offering a range of courses from basic literacy to high school equivalency at an off-site education center that is run in conjunction with the local school district and technical college. At the same time, the firm has expanded its internal training program for machine operators, moving from an informal system to one that involves a combination of classroom and structured on-the-job training.

Apparel

Even such traditionally labor-intensive industries as apparel manufacturing have been affected by the need to speed production. In traditional apparel-making systems, production is split up into dozens of operations, each performed by a different operator. Workers usually have bundles containing up to sixty pieces beside their workstations. Thus each operation is protected from problems occurring in other operations (and employers can continue to use piece rates), but garments that may need only a few minutes of work can take many days to wend their way through the plant.

In order to speed production, managers have developed systems—referred to as sewing modules—in which pieces are passed directly from operator to operator. As in all attempts to reduce in-process inventory, this removes the buffers that prevent problems in one area from spreading to others.

Although the actual sewing tasks carried out by workers in modules do not differ from the tasks performed by bundle workers, the module system requires fundamental changes in the industry's human resource practices. Supervisors and engineers can no longer focus on workers in isolation but must consider the effect of the action of each worker and of the design of each task on the simultaneous functioning of the group. Workers themselves must become involved in the quality and pace of production of their coworkers. Theoretically, if one operator falls behind, then another group member will help catch up. In well-functioning modules, any imbalances in the production process will be corrected in this way without any intervention by the supervisor. This obviously requires some of the operators to be able to do a variety of tasks.

Machine maintenance and repair are much more important in modules than in the bundle system, since a machine breakdown can quickly stop the entire group. One manager estimated that each minute that a sewing machine was out of service cost $3 to $4. In one shirt plant, the managers plan to teach the operators some of the basics of machine maintenance and repair so that the operators can repair small problems or at least have some sense of the cause of a problem when a mechanic arrives to correct it.

Mechanics too must have a deeper and more abstract knowledge of the equipment. For example, when one large firm first installed some sophisticated semi-automatic equipment, the management expected that their mechanics would have trouble with the advanced electronic and hydraulic components. And indeed they did. But the managers also found that the mechanics had a poor understanding of the sewing components that they had been repairing for years. Previously, they could take their time in repairing a broken machine, using a trial-and-error method. If that did not work, they could take the machine out of service and tinker around with it until they got it going. Their knowledge was entirely experience-based. As one manager put it succinctly, "Those mechanics couldn't fix a thing that they hadn't fixed before." Without buffer inventories, broken machines quickly lead to downstream disruptions. One company has dealt with this problem by developing training procedures designed to give mechanics a much more sophisticated knowledge of all components of the machines they have to work with. The catalyst for change was as much the new system of production as the nature of the new equipment.

EVIDENCE OF CHANGING WORK AND SKILLS

The measurement of skills has proved to be extremely difficult. Direct observation of work tasks is costly and may focus on the skills that are available rather than those that are optimal for the effective performance of the tasks. Moreover, there is no accepted conceptualization of skills or widely used methodology for measuring them. In the absence of a direct measure of changing skill requirements, analysts must use logical or theoretical arguments as well as a variety of indirect measures to attempt to understand the changing nature of work.

So far we have made a two-step conceptual argument. First, we have argued that firms are adopting more flexible production processes in the face of a rapidly changing and uncertain economic environment. Second, we have suggested that flexible production systems that can respond to the intensified pace of change require higher-skilled workers. We now present evidence in support of these two propositions.

The spread of innovative work organization

Information on the shift from traditional to more flexible and innovative work organization comes from focused case studies as well as broader surveys. Each will be discussed below.

Case studies. Most of the information about the spread of innovative work organization comes from case studies. Production systems that rely more on the active initiative and contributions of lower-skilled members of the work force are spreading through-out the domestic auto industry (Katz, 1985; Womack, Jones, & Roos, 1990). Banks have used distributed data processing to decentralize authority to branches. In the early 1970s, U.S. banks gave only limited responsibilities to their branches—basically to service routine contacts with individual customers—which in any case involved a limited number of products and services. The branches had no control over back office processing or loan approvals. Now, however, to create better links to specific markets and customers, banks have moved towards decentralizing loan, investment, and marketing decisions to groups of branches. This has been accompanied by an increase in responsibility for some branch employees who, rather than simply signing clients up for a limited number of services, are expected to help clients choose from among a much larger portfolio of products (Bertrand & Noyelle, 1988).

The trend towards decentralization of organization and decision making is evident within many plants in the textile and apparel industries. Since the mid-1980s, as style changes in apparel and textiles have accelerated, leaders in those industries have turned from a virtual obsession with automation to an equally strong preoccupation with the Quick Response strategy, which is designed to reduce production and delivery times. While Quick Response involves a reformulation of the links between producers, suppliers, and retailers, organizational reform is also an important component. Industry organizations such as the American Apparel Manufacturers Association (AAMA) have been advocating the use of teamwork in apparel production rather than the traditional system that emphasizes work fragmentation and hierarchical control.

To assess the spread of new production techniques, the American Apparel Manufacturers Association conducted a survey of its members in 1989. In 1985, only one percent of the production workers in the firms that responded to the survey were being used in production processes designed to reduce in-process inventory and speed throughput times. By 1988, that share had risen to 7 percent, and according to plans current when the survey was conducted, 20 percent would be used by the early 1990s (AAMA, 1989, pp. 3-4).

In general, reports from the field suggest that there has been a significant increase in decentralizing work during the last decade. Kochan, Cutcher-Gershenfeld, and MacDuffie, in their 1989 review of work reform, concluded that a variety of evidence supports "the conclusion that both activity and interest in these issues [workplace innovation] has escalated to unprecedented levels" (p. 1834).

Survey data. Although the case studies suggest a growing interest in innovative work organization, they fail to provide a precise sense of the overall spread of work reform. This type of information must come from sample surveys of firm practices, but results from surveys have not been definitive. This is to a large extent a methodological problem. Most survey-based information about work comes from individuals rather than firms. It would be most appropriate to gather information about work reform directly from firms, but existing surveys have almost nothing about work organization or human resource policies. Even for those that do, there is no accepted definition or measurement of work reform. Techniques such as teamwork, labor management committees, employee involvement, decentralization, and worker empowerment can each involve either insignificant or profound changes. In any case, the most significant organizational innovations may no longer be seen as special features. To the extent that these efforts are seen as "programs" or "experiments," they are probably not well integrated into the operation of the firm. For all of these reasons, answers to survey questions that could be used to measure the spread of work reform are difficult to interpret.

Nevertheless, the number of surveys that provide relevant information is growing. A 1982 study by the New York Stock Exchange reported that 44 percent of the responding firms used some form of quality circle. Moreover, three-fourths of these efforts were less than two years old (New York Stock Exchange, 1982). A 1985 *Business Week*-sponsored survey found that 36 percent of respondents had some form of employee participation project underway (Alper, Pfau, & Sirota, 1985). And a 1988 study of large employers found that about half reported an employee participation program. Responses to retrospective questions revealed that almost all of this activity had started since 1980 (Ichniowski, Lewin, & Delaney, 1988). Another study found that about 50 percent of unionized manufacturing firms had some type of joint participation scheme and that most of them were started in the 1980s (Voos, 1987).

The most comprehensive survey was conducted by the General Accounting Office in 1988. This was a survey of the Fortune 1000 and achieved about a 47 percent response rate. Firms were asked to report what percentage of their workers were involved in several different types of innovative organizational programs such as profit sharing, employee stock ownership plans, teams, quality circles, and others. For this group of companies, the proportion of workers working in these programs varied from less than 10 percent to closer to 50 percent, but once again, the data suggested strong growth of innovative strategies in the 1980s (Eaton & Voos, 1991).

The evidence for the spread of innovative work organization remains suggestive at best. Precise estimates of the number of firms or workers involved in work reform or the depth, significance, and effectiveness of the programs that do exist are not possible. Perhaps the most that can be said about their spread is that a significant minority of larger firms do appear to be involved with some form of work reform or employee involvement. However, there is no question that tremendous resistance to fundamental reform persists. Many employee involvement efforts are superficial or even manipulative. Unless they are faced with severe economic problems, most employers are not likely to take human resource changes very far.

On the other hand, the case study work combined with the survey results allows us to conclude that there has been an important growth of interest in new approaches to human resource management in the production process. Given the past success of the mass production system and the strong commitment that American managers have had to traditional labor-saving automation and to the rationalization and deskilling of the remaining jobs, the changes that can be observed suggest that the underlying forces pushing firms towards work reform must be strong.

Education, skills, and the pace of economic change

If workplaces are becoming more flexible and less well-defined, then what implications does that have for skill requirements? Research does suggest that educated workers are better able to cope with change and uncertainty. In the mid-1970s, Charles Schultz (1979) argued that education improved a worker's ability to deal with "disequilibria." And as Levin suggested in 1987, the same logic suggests that workers with higher educational levels are able to operate more effectively than those with less education in decentralized work settings with high levels of employee involvement. In a 1987 study, Bartel and Lichtenberg found that the average educational level of an industry's work force tended to be higher in industries with newer equipment. Industries with newer equipment are likely to be those in which the technology has changed recently. This suggests that if on average the pace of technology increases, then there will be a general increase in the demand for higher-educated workers.

Information on training provided by firms also confirms the relationship between the pace of change and the quantity of training.   Japanese auto companies have been much more successful than U.S. companies in accelerating the pace of model change, and Higuchi (1987) found that Japanese plants in the U.S. provide more training than the U.S. plants of U.S. companies.   A comprehensive study of the automobile industry (Womack, Jones, & Roos, 1990) found a similar relationship between product innovation and training. Other research has also related productivity change with training. Although productivity may change for many reasons (for example, increased plant utilization rates), it is likely that firms or industries experiencing faster productivity growth will also be characterized by changes in production processes and technologies. Thus Mincer and Higuchi (1988) found that increases in productivity in Japanese manufacturing firms were also associated with increases in firm-based training. And research by Tan (1989) reveals a positive relationship between average productivity change in an industry and the amount of firm-based training.

INDIRECT MEASURES OF SKILL CHANGE

In this section we turn to two additional types of empirical evidence that suggest that skill requirements are increasing: changes in relative wage rates and shifting occupational patterns.[1]

---

[1]Many studies use the U.S. Department of Labor *Dictionary of Occupational Titles* (DOT) to examine changes in the skills needed within occupations. The DOT was designed to survey periodically the changing characteristics of

Changing relative wages

Changes in wages earned by different groups of workers show a steady increase in the demand for workers with higher levels of education. In 1979, full-time 25-to-34-year-old male workers with college degrees earned about 13 percent more than similar high school graduates. The earnings differential for these groups rose to 38 percent by 1987. For women in the same age group, the premium earned by college graduates rose from 23 percent in 1979 to 45 percent in 1987 (Levy & Murnane, in press, table 7).

This increasing educational wage gap suggests that the demand for higher-educated workers is rising relative to the demand for workers with less education. If the jobs that employers have to offer now "require" more skills, then employers would be willing to offer more money to attract adequately skilled workers.

Changing demand is not the only influence on wages. Changes in supply will also affect earnings levels. Indeed, in the 1980s there was a decline in the growth rate of college graduates, and a sharp drop in the supply of college graduates could have driven up their wages even without any changes in demand. But this supply factor cannot explain the entire wage gap. This is especially true in manufacturing. If the rising wage gap had been caused primarily by a shrinking of the relative supply of college

---

thousands of individual occupations. The last update was carried out in 1977. Unfortunately, any conclusions about changing characteristics derived from these data are made unreliable by methodological problems. Neither the DOT's list of occupations nor its occupational definitions were fully updated. Hence, many of the newest occupations or suboccupations are simply missing, and between three-quarters and four-fifths of the descriptions are identical in the last two rounds of the survey (Spenner, 1983). Kenneth Spenner's (1985) review of this research suggests, if anything, a slight overall tendency toward upgrading skills, despite the bias that these data have against change.

graduates, then manufacturing employers would have hired fewer college graduates and more high school graduates, but the data show a relative shift towards the higher-educated group. The employment of full-time 25-to-34-year-old college graduates rose by 10 percent between 1979 and 1987, while their earnings rose by one-third. In contrast, the employment of high school graduates in the same age group in manufacturing rose by only 6 percent, while their earnings *fell* by 11 percent (Levy & Murnane, in press, table 9). Thus in their review of the large and growing body of research on the shifting patterns of relative wages, Levy and Murnane conclude that during the 1980s there was a steady rise in the relative demand for more highly educated workers.

Shifting occupational structure

Occupational data also show a steady relative rise in the employment of workers in occupations that tend to be filled by individuals with higher educational levels. Moreover, the occupational data understate the magnitude of the shift towards higher-educated workers.

Much of the controversy concerning skills has involved discussions of changes in the occupational distribution. Occupational categories have a concrete meaning to most people. A decline in the number of laborers and maids accompanied by an increase in the number of computer analysts, nurses, and engineers suggests in a concrete and understandable way that overall skill and educational needs have increased.

In the industries that we have studied, this type of shift does appear to be taking place. For example, in the financial service sector in the United States, managers, professionals, and sales workers accounted for 47 percent of employment in 1971 and 52 percent in 1985. Automatic teller machines and the computerization of back-office functions have eliminated many of the lowest-level clerical and teller positions in banking. In the textile industry, there were 4.2 operatives, laborers, and service workers for every craft and technical worker in 1975, but by 1985 this ratio had fallen to 3.5 to one. In apparel, the ratio of repair technicians to operators has grown, although operator positions continue to account for the overwhelming majority of nonmanagerial jobs in the industry. For example, at one apparel firm, there were approximately 12 sewing machine mechanics for 2,400 operators in the 1970s, whereas there were 40 mechanics for 1,200 operators in 1988.

Table 1 is based on data on the growth of nine all-inclusive broad occupational categories between 1975 and 1990. The first group of occupational categories all have average educational levels, measured by the share of the workers in the occupation with at least some college, above the average for the economy as a whole. Since the mid-1970s, as a group, these higher-level occupations have grown at almost two-and-one-half times the rate of the lower-skilled jobs, and although they still accounted for less than 40 percent of employment in 1990, more than one-half of all net employment growth between 1975 and 1990 took place within the higher-skill occupations.

But what about trends between now and the year 2005? Proponents of the argument that skills will fall frequently point out that forecasts suggest that some occupations generally considered to require little skill will add large numbers of jobs to the economy over the next decade. The ten occupations that are projected to add the most jobs to the economy by the year 2005, with the exception of registered nurses and general managers, all generally require low skills. The remaining eight lower-skill occupations among these ten account for about one-fifth of the total job growth between 1990 and 2005.

Although tales of the proliferation of fast-food workers and janitors have had a strong influence on public opinion, looking at absolute growth in particular occupations can be misleading.

Large occupational categories with low rates of growth can still add many jobs. Indeed since low-skill jobs are less differentiated than higher-skill jobs, lower-skill jobs tend to be categorized in large groups.

Table 1. Changes in the Occupational Structure, 1975-1990

Occupations[1]	Number of Jobs 1990 (000)	Percent Distribution	Percent[2] Growth 1975-1990	Percent[3] of Job Growth 1975-1990
Group 1[4] Prof. Specialty Occs. Tech. & Rel. Support Exec., Admin., & Manag. Marketing & Sales	46,543	38%	65%	56%
Group 2[5] Administrative Support Service Occupations Prec., Prodctn., & Craft Ag., For., & Fish. Op., Fab., & Laborers	76,030	62%	24%	44%
TOTAL	122,573	100%	37%	100%

Source: Silvestri & Lukasiewicz, 1991, Table 1.
          Educational levels are from unpublished data provided by the BLS.

[1]Full Names of Occupations:
    Prof. Specialty Occs.-------- Professional Specialty Occupations
    Tech. & Rel. Support--------- Technicians and Related Support Occupations
    Exec., Admin., & Manag.--- Executive, Administrative, and Managerial
    Marketing & Sales------------ Marketing and Sales Occupations
    Administrative Support------- Administrative Support Occupations (Including Clerical)
    Service Occupations---------- Service Occupations
    Prec., Prdctn., & Craft------ Precision, Production, Craft, and Repair
    Ag., For., & Fish.----------- Agriculture, Forestry, and Fishery and Related
    Op., Fab., & Laborers-------- Operators, Fabricators, and Laborers

[2]Percent growth for each occupational group.

[3]Percent of the nation's total job growth by each occupational group.

[4]Occupations in Group 1 are those in which the percentage of individuals with at least one year of postsecondary education is higher than for the work force as a whole.

[5]Occupations in Group 2 are those in which the percentage of individuals with at least one year of postsecondary education is lower than for the work force as a whole.

The list of the fastest-growing jobs is dominated by occupations characterized by middle-level skills. Thus paralegals, system analysts and computer scientists, physical therapists, medical assistants, operations research analysts, human services workers, radiologic technologists, and medical secretaries are all among the top ten. But this approach can also be criticized, since fast-growing occupations can start from extremely low bases and therefore will contribute few actual jobs. The ten fastest-growing occupations account for less than 6 percent of the total projected net job growth by 2005 (Silvestri & Lukasiewicz, 1991, Table 4).

These problems can be avoided by looking at the occupational structure as a whole rather than focusing on selected jobs. Table 2 divides the occupational structure into the higher- and lower-level occupational categories that were used earlier in Table 1. The trend towards higher skills that has characterized the last 15 years will continue, although projections suggest that the trend may be somewhat weaker. Between 1975 and 1990, the higher-skill occupations grew two-and-a-half times as fast as the lower-skill. During the 15 years between 1990 and 2005, they are expected to grow just under twice as fast.

Table 3 extends this analysis by presenting data on the implications of these occupational projections for the distribution of education in the year 2005. The analysis is carried out as follows: First, the projected growth rates are used to calculate the total projected number of jobs in each occupational category. Then the distribution of 1990 incumbents in each occupation among the four educational groups is applied to that total. For example, if 44 percent of the managers in 1990 had a college degree, it is assumed that in 2005, 44 percent will still have a college degree. This yields a year 2005 projection for the number of workers in each occupational category who are also in each educational group. Next, taking all of the occupations, the numbers in each educational category are summed, giving a projection for the total number of workers in each educational group. Thus any change in the distribution of education results *only* from the differential growth rates of the occupations. This is an assumption with a strong bias against change, since it assumes that no change takes place within each occupation.

Table 2.

Projected Changes in Occupational Structure, 1990-2005

Occupations	Number of Jobs 1990 (000)	Percent Distribution	Percent[1] Growth 1990-2005	Percent[2] of Job Growth 1990-2005	Educational Level[3]
Group 1[4] Prof. Specialty Occs. Tech. & Rel. Support Exec., Admin., & Manag. Marketing & Sales	46,543	38%	22%	55%	69%
Group 2[5] Administrative Support Service Occupations Prec., Prodctn., & Craft Ag., For., & Fish. Op., Fab., & Laborers	76,030	62%	13%	45%	27%
TOTAL	122,573	100%	19%	100%	43%

Source: Silvestri & Lukasiewicz, 1991, Table 1.
            Educational levels are from unpublished data provided by the BLS.

See Table 1 for the complete names of the occupations.

[1]Percent growth for each occupational group.

[2]Percent of the nation's total job growth by each occupational group.

[3]The percent of all individuals employed in this occupation who have completed at least one year of postsecondary education.

[4]Occupations in Group 1 are those in which the percentage of individuals with at least one year of postsecondary education is higher than for the work force as a whole.

[5]Occupations in Group 2 are those in which the percentage of individuals with at least one year of postsecondary education is lower than for the work force as a whole.

Table 3. Projected Occupational Growth & Education

	Amount of Total Employment Held by Workers With:				
	<H.S. (000)	H.S. (000)	1.3 Yr. Col. (000)	4 + Yr. Col. (000)	Total (000)
Jobs in 1990	20,587	49,157	25,327	27,184	122,573[1]
Percentages	17%	40%	21%	22%	100%
Jobs in 2005	23,992	57,688	30,587	34,555	147,192
Percentages	16%	39%	21%	24%	100%
Net new jobs, 1990-2005	3,404	8,530	5,260	7,371	24,566
Percentages	14%	35%	21%	30%	100%

Source: Silvestri & Lukasiewicz, 1991, Table 1.
Educational levels are from unpublished data provided by the BLS.

[1]Variations in the Total column are due to rounding error.

Despite this conservative bias, the analysis suggests that the new jobs that are expected to be created over the next decade will have higher educational levels than current jobs. For example, 17 percent of the 1990 jobs were filled by workers who have not completed 12 years of school, while this share for new jobs created by 2005 will be 14 percent. The discrepancy between current jobs and new jobs for college graduates is even larger. According to this calculation, college graduates hold 22 percent of the current jobs, while 30 percent of the new jobs will go to workers who have completed four years of college. Moreover, judging from the record of past projections, this is probably an underestimate of the relative growth of those occupations filled by workers with higher educational levels.[2]

Although the occupational projections give a more concrete understanding of trends in the nature of work, they also have serious weaknesses. In particular, they cannot take into account any changes within occupations. The methodologies used to forecast educational needs based on occupational projections assume that the educational requirements of all occupations do not change—that the only source of change is the different rates of growth of different occupations. In other words, it is assumed that the job of a secretary or repair mechanic will not change between the base year, 1990, and the forecast year, 2005. Thus the overall effects depend very much on the growth rate of employment, which the Bureau of Labor Statistics projects will be 20 percent between 1990 and 2005. An approach to understanding changing job requirements that *assumes* that more than that 80 percent of the jobs have not changed has obvious limitations.

---

[2]For a detailed discussion of the use of occupational projections for the analysis of changing skill needs, see Bailey, 1991.

SKILL IMPLICATIONS

The changing economic environment has pushed firms towards important changes in the ways that they organize work and production processes. These changes have implications for the work activities of both production workers and higher-level workers such as supervisors, managers, and professionals.

Production workers

The quantity and quality of education and training for front-line workers must be upgraded, but the content must also be changed. All of the empirical evidence that we have reviewed suggests that many production workers have an increasing need for the types of skills traditionally learned in school—literacy, arithmetic, and at a higher level, specific technical knowledge. But the case studies in particular suggest that current changes in work call for more than simply an increase in traditional education. On the job, diverse tasks have been combined in new ways and even low-level workers have been given new responsibilities. Thus educational reform should look beyond the quantity of education. The content of education needs to be brought more in line with the types of activities students will be engaged in after they leave school. What types of skills, then, are needed in the emerging workplace?

Workers increasingly need to be able to operate more independently of their supervision and to work in a less well-defined environment. This requires a greater facility for creative thinking, decision making, reasoning, and problem solving. Workers need to have a broader understanding of the systems in which they operate. Without this, they are much less able to make decisions about their own activities. Nor will they be able to monitor and correct the performance of those systems or to participate in the improvement of their design. This was not an issue when they were simply expected to follow instruction; their role within the broader operations of their organization was the concern of their supervisors and managers.

But even more than a broader knowledge of their context, they need a more abstract or conceptual understanding of what they are doing. This is what allows them to carry out tasks or solve problems that they have not encountered before or that they have not been shown specifically how to carry out or solve. Thus, more than in the past, individuals will need to be able to acquire, organize, and interpret information. Workers will also have more direct interaction with their coworkers, and therefore will need more experience in general social skills such as group problem solving and negotiation. These changes clearly involve more than an accumulation of the type of knowledge traditionally learned in schools.

Most of the discussion about skill deficiencies has focused on the education and training of lower-level workers, or the "non-college bound." Indeed, if lower-level jobs are either being eliminated or are being transformed to require broader and deeper skills, then the changing nature of work has perhaps its most obvious effects on this strata of workers. Nevertheless, we do not conclude from this that all students should try to earn four-year college degrees. In the next chapter, we shall address the problem of pedagogical reform at all levels of schooling. We believe that this is more important at this stage than an attempt to put everyone through college.

Managerial and higher level workers

Although the problems of the non-college-bound have received most of the attention, changes in the nature of work have important implications for the training and education of managerial and professional workers. Indeed, there is widespread complacency about the quality of baccalaureate education in the US, at least as it compares to such education abroad. The educational policy problem is almost always conceptualized as a crisis for the non-college-bound. But the link between the changes in educational needs and the way in which work is organized suggests that higher-level workers will not escape the effects of these changes. Managers accustomed to taking instructions from above and passing them to subordinates will have to learn to operate in a much more interactive environment. They might be expected to take initiative outside of their traditional areas of responsibility, but they may also have to learn to work with subordinates who take a more active role than they did before. The spread of knowledge and responsibility more widely throughout an organization alters power and authority.

To combat the traditional fragmentation of work, some firms have begun to blur the distinction between departments and functions. Whereas design, engineering, production, finance, marketing, and customer service departments previously worked sequentially or in isolation from each other, some companies are now using teams with representatives from all of these functions. These cross-functional teams expose managers and professionals to a wide set of activities, and if they are to participate effectively, they must also have broader knowledge. The educational preparation of an engineer or finance specialist might be very different if he or she could expect to have constant interactions with others who previously carried out separate and usually nonoverlapping functions.

So far, in comparison to research on the educational needs of front-line workers, there has been much less research concerning the ways in which the roles and educational requirements of higher-level workers have changed. Therefore, at this stage our conclusion is based primarily on the observation that these workers could not have escaped the effects of work reform.

Nevertheless, the current widespread dissatisfaction with education in business schools is certainly consistent with our conjectures. The traditional Master of Business Administration program emphasized specialized technical skills. Students were taught that management was a science and that decisions could be made on the basis of well-defined analytic techniques. But critics of this approach now argue that the overspecialization of the typical MBA program is not appropriate for the current business environment. Much greater emphasis must be placed on broader knowledge and interdisciplinary training. Executives might still specialize in finance, but they also need to have some understanding of other aspects of the operation, such as marketing, production, customer service, and product and service development. This broadening of required knowledge and skepticism about the wisdom of superspecialization is strikingly consistent with the types of changes being advocated for lower-level positions as well.

CONCLUSION

In this chapter, we have reviewed several different types of empirical evidence, including case studies, broader statistical research relating education to economic change, occupational data, and studies of the changing wage structure. The consistency of the implications of all this evidence strengthens the overall picture of a rising demand for higher-skilled and more-educated labor. It is important to consider all these various sources because the weaknesses of one type of evidence can be overcome by the strengths of other types.

For example, the wage analysis provides a compelling picture of the overall shift in the demand for workers with different levels of education, but fails to give a more concrete picture of the types of skills that are increasingly in demand or the causes of those increases. The occupational data do develop a more readily understandable picture of some aspects of the changes in work, but current occupational data require that the analysis be carried out using the assumption that the content of each job remains the same. Certainly the examples that we have presented suggest that this assumption severely limits the value of the analysis based on occupational data. Moreover, both the educational classifications on which the wage analysis is based and the occupational categorizations on which the occupational analysis is based are crude measures of skills. The case studies can provide just the type of concrete understanding, both across and within occupations, in which the more aggregate approaches are weakest. But the wage and occupational data do provide comprehensive results, while the generalizability of case studies is always open to question. Thus a more powerful case can be built using all of the types of evidence than could emerge from just one approach.

Finally, in addition to the direct empirical evidence on the changing demand for higher-educated workers, we have presented a logical argument based on the nature of the underlying economic environment. Thus we have shown that change, variety, and uncertainty have increased; that those changes call for innovations in work organization and production processes; and that those innovations require a higher-skilled work force.

In the following chapters we shall develop the concept of effective learning. The ideas that underlie our understanding of effective learning have emerged for the most part from recent advances in cognitive psychology and learning theory and therefore appear to be independent of changes in the economy. Nevertheless, effective learning environments as we understand them are also consistent with the emerging needs of the economy.

3

INEFFECTIVE LEARNING

The nature of work has changed, and our understanding of how people learn has also changed. Both developments call into question the organization, goals, and pedagogy of our educational system. What makes these developments so powerful is that our new understanding of both work and learning suggest very similar directions for reform. Strengthening the educational system so that it conforms more to the ways that people learn will also directly enhance the ability of that system to prepare students for the types of workplaces that are emerging in factories and offices throughout the country.

Our discussion of effective learning emerges from a powerful knowledge base known as cognitive science. Using the lens of cognitive science, this chapter makes two basic points about learning and teaching. First, school routinely and profoundly violates what we know about how people learn effectively and the conditions under which they apply their knowledge appropriately to new situations. Second, these practices seem to permeate all levels and sectors of American education and training, from elementary grades to corporate training.

Linking this argument to the last chapter's discussion of the economy, we make two other points. First, during the mass production era in the U.S. economy, these traditional educational practices were relatively consistent with how work was organized for those in lower-skill jobs. And they did not appear to impose any particular cost on those who filled higher-skill jobs. Second, pressures on U.S. industries and their effects on the organization of work alter the payoffs of traditionally organized learning. These practices are now inconsistent with the skills required in restructured workplaces, regardless of the level of the job.

FIVE ASSUMPTIONS ABOUT LEARNING: ALL WRONG

Mistaken assumption #1: The educational enterprise assumes that people predictably transfer learning to new situations

As a society, we presume that the ultimate point of schooling is to prepare students for effective and responsible functioning outside of the school. Accepting this assumption means that we have to confront what is known as the "knowledge transfer problem." *Knowledge transfer* simply means the appropriate use in a new situation of concepts, skills, knowledge, and strategies acquired in another.

Historically, lower-skilled workers had a very limited need for transfer. Transfer becomes important when you encounter the unfamiliar and nonroutine, and lower-skilled workers encountered little that was not familiar and did not have responsibility for handling the nonroutine that they did encounter. Goods and services were limited in number, allowing long production runs of the same thing or service and reducing the number of previously unencountered events. Within this limited product or service range, companies organized the work as "specialist" work—workers had responsibility for a narrow range of activity. Supervisors and managers were expected to handle the nonroutine events that did occur within this narrow, repetitive world. In other words, responsibility for events that required problem solving, judgment, heuristics, analogues, or other mental activities enhanced by access to knowledge and skills acquired in other situations was detached from lower-skill jobs and vested in middle-skill managerial jobs.

However, increased change, documented in the previous chapter, means an increased number of nonroutine events. U.S. companies are gradually shifting from highly specialized and repetitive jobs at lower skill levels toward teams expected to handle a broader range of activities, and they are also increasingly vesting problem-solving, supervisory responsibilities in these teams. Thus, a broader range of workers is being asked to exercise the mental activities enhanced by access to knowledge and skills acquired in other situations.

Extensive research, spanning decades, shows that individuals do not predictably transfer knowledge in any of three situations where transfer should occur. They do not predictably transfer school knowledge to everyday practice (e.g., Pea, 1989; Lave, 1988a). They do not predictably transfer sound everyday practice to school endeavors, even when the former seems clearly relevant to the latter. They do not predictably transfer their learning across school subjects. We focus on the first two transfer problems: from school to nonschool and from nonschool to school.

Transferring from school to outside of school. This transfer situation is at the heart of schooling. Usually the major claim for school-type instruction is its generality and power of transfer to situations beyond the classroom (Resnick, 1987). The fundamental question is whether knowledge, skills, and strategies acquired in formal education in fact get used appropriately in everyday practice.

Students in college physics courses designed for physics majors can solve "book" problems in Newtonian mechanics by rote application of formulae. However, even after instruction, they revert to naive pre-Newtonian explanations of common physical situations to which their school learning is relevant (diSessa, 1983).

Studies of expert radiologists, electronic trouble-shooters, and lawyers all reveal a surprising lack of transfer of theoretical principles, processes, or skills learned in school to professional practice (Resnick, 1987). For example, Morris and Rouse (1985) found that extensive training in electronics and troubleshooting theories provided little knowledge and fewer skills directly applicable to performing electronic troubleshooting.

Transferring from outside of school to school. People learn outside of school all the time. In fact, Piaget's point that intelligence is built out of interaction with the environment is really a point that learning opportunities are "thick on the ground." The question then is what people do with what they learn outside of school when they move into school. Does sound, everyday practice get transferred to—get used in—school learning? How does "incorrect" learning outside school affect "correct" learning inside school?

Dairy workers, although almost errorless in their use of practical arithmetic at work, performed badly on arithmetic tests with problems like those encountered in their jobs (Scribner & Fahrmeir, 1982). Brazilian street vendor children successfully solved 98 percent of their marketplace transactions, such as calculating total costs and change. When presented with the same transactions in formal arithmetic word problems that provided some descriptive context, the children correctly solved 74 percent of the problems. Their success rate dropped to 37 percent when asked to solve the same types of problems when these were presented as mathematical operations without descriptive context (Carraher, Carraher, & Schliemann, 1985).

Herndon (1971, as quoted in Lave, 1988a), a middle school teacher working with students who had failed in mainstream classrooms, discovered that one of his students had a well-paid regular job scoring for a bowling league. The work demanded fast, accurate, complicated arithmetic:

> eight bowling scores at once. Adding quickly, not making any mistakes (for no one was going to put up with errors), following the rather complicated process of scoring in the game of bowling. Get a spare, score ten plus whatever you get on the next ball, score a strike, then ten plus whatever you get on the next two balls; imagine the man gets three strikes in a row and two spares and you are the scorer, plus you are dealing with seven other guys all striking or sparing or neither one.

> I figured I had this particular...kid now. Back in eighth period I lectured him on how smart he was to be a league scorer in bowling. I pried admissions from the other boys, about how they had paper routes and made change. I made the girls confess that when they went to buy stuff they didn't have any difficulty deciding if those shoes cost $10.95 or whether it meant $109.50 or whether it meant $1.09 or how much change they'd get back from a twenty. Naturally I then handed out bowling-score problems, and naturally everyone could choose which ones they wanted to solve, and naturally the result was that all the...kids immediately rushed me yelling "Is this right? I don't know how to do it! What's the answer? This ain't right, is it?" and "What's my grade?" The girls who bought shoes for $10.95 with a $20 bill came up with $400.15 for change and wanted to know if that was right? The brilliant league scorer couldn't decide whether two strikes and a third frame of eight amounted to eighteen or twenty-eight or whether it was one hundred and eight and a half (p. 66).

Lave (1988a) reports a very low relationship between success in arithmetic tests and correct solutions to best-buy calculations in the supermarket. An analysis of the data shows discontinuities in performances, errors, and procedures between the supermarket on one hand and test activities on the other, although the arithmetic problems are formally similar and the persons solving them the same.

Other studies show that training on one version of a logical problem has little, if any, effect on solving an isomorphic version that is represented differently (Hayes & Simon, 1977). Teaching children to use general context-independent cognitive strategies has no clear benefits outside the specific domains in which they are taught (Pressley, Snyder, & Cariaglia-Bull, 1987, as cited in Perkins & Salomon, 1989).

Conclusion. Cognitive experts agree that the conditions for transfer are not fully understood. Even though the recent studies cited in the previous paragraph continue to find no evidence of transfer, others identify conditions under which transfer seems to occur (e.g., Holyoak, 1985; Novick, 1988; Nisbett, Fong, Lehman, & Cheng, 1987; Lehman, Lempert, & Nisbett, 1988; Singley & Anderson, 1989). We know that people routinely apply skills such as reading, writing, and arithmetic to new situations with some success. These skills are used most effectively in well-understood content domains. For example, readers get more out of their reading when they know something about the domain in which they are reading than when they do not. Nonetheless, skills such as reading do let us "enter" unfamiliar content areas —we do use these skills in new situations, and they do help us.

At the same time, we also keep finding lack of transfer. We now know that certain practices of schools impede learning. More effective learning may not be sufficient for transfer, but poor initial learning will certainly impede it. The next four "mistakes" are really about educational practices that inadvertently create learning problems and thus transfer problems.

Mistaken assumption #2: Learners are best seen as passive vessels into which knowledge is poured

Think about a typical schoolroom, or a Congressional hearing, or a corporate training session. The teacher—or "expert"—faces the learners in the role of knowledge source. The learner is the passive receiver of wisdom—a glass into which water is poured.

This instructional arrangement comes out of an implicit assumption about the basic purpose of education: the transmission of the society's culture from one generation to the next. The concept of transmission implies a one-way flow from the adult members of the society to the society's young (Lave, 1988b)—or from the expert to the novice.

In fact, schooling is often talked about as the transmission of "canonical" knowledge—in other words, of an authoritative, structured body of principles, rules, and knowledge. Education as canonical transmission thus becomes the conveying of what experts know to be true, rather than a process of inquiry, discovery, and wonder. This view of education leads naturally to the student as receiver of the word, to a lecture mode of teaching, and to the teacher as the controller of the process.

This organization of learning, with the teacher as order-giver and the student as order-taker, fits the traditional organization of work for lower-skilled workers in both civilian workplaces and the military. "The worker's...responsibility was...to do what he was told [to do by management]" (Callahan, 1962, p. 27). Ben Hamper, an auto assembly line worker, uses more colorful language: "Working the line at G.M. was like being paid to flunk high school for the rest of your life" (Marchese, 1991, p. 32).

To some extent it also fits how work was organized for higher-level personnel in large, bureaucratic American companies.

William Whyte's classic study *The Organization Man* (1956) portrays middle- and higher-level workers as order-takers as well as order-transmitters.

The assumption that the teacher is the pourer and the student the receptacle has several unfortunate consequences.

Passive learning reduces or removes chances for exploration, discovery, and invention. Passive learning means that learners do not interact with problems and content and thus do not get the experiential feedback that is key to learning. Students need chances to engage in choice, judgment, control processes, and problem formulation; they need chances to make mistakes. The saying, "experience is the best teacher," is borne out by the research—you learn when you do. While not sufficient for effective learning, doing is nonetheless necessary.

However, schools usually present what is to be learned as a delineated body of knowledge, with the result that students come to regard the subject being studied—mathematics, for example—as something received, not discovered, and as an entity to be ingested, rather than as a form of activity, argumentation, and social discourse.

This organization of learning mirrors the traditional organization of work, especially for lower-skilled workers. Under the system of industrial management known as "scientific management" or the "Taylor System," "each man's task was worked out by the planning department. Each worker received an instruction card which described in minute detail 'not only what is to be done, but how it is to be done and the exact time allowed for doing it'" (Callahan, 1962, p. 31). This system was highly prescriptive; it left no room for deviation or innovation.

Passive learning places control over learning in the teacher's, not the learner's, hands. Passive learning creates learners dependent on teachers for guidance and feedback, thus undercutting the development of confidence in their own sense-making abilities, their initiative, and their cognitive executive skills.

Recall Herndon's students. They were asked to solve school math problems like ones that they had mastered outside of school. The problems were even presented in contexts that they had already mastered outside of school. Their responses revealed that they had no sense of control over school problems. They guessed wildly, ran to Herndon for confirmation and help, and showed no confidence that their nonschool experiences could help them.

Recall the Brazilian street vendor children. The researchers found that when the children tried to work school math problems, they did not check the sensibleness of their answers by relating them back to the initial problem. Although virtually errorless in their street math activities, they came up with results for school math problems as preposterous as those of Herndon's students (Carraher, et al., 1985).

In the study of supermarket shoppers' use of arithmetic, the researchers assessed the shoppers' command of structurally similar school math problems. The shoppers spoke with self-deprecation about not having studied math for a long time. Common requests were "May I rewrite problems?" and "Should I...?"

Lave (1988a) clarifies what is happening here. Individuals experience themselves as both subjects and objects in the world. In the supermarket, for example, they see themselves as controlling "their activities, interacting with the setting, generating problems in relation [to] the setting, and controlling problem-solving processes. In contrast, school...create[s] contexts in which children...experience themselves as objects, with no control over problems or choice about problem-solving processes" (pp. 69-70). In sum, control in the teachers', not the students', hands undercuts students' trust in their own sense-making abilities.

Anecdotes tell us that control in the hands of supervisors in traditionally organized workplaces imposes the same costs on workers as control in the hands of teachers imposes on students. As companies have started shifting decision-making power to the shop floor, managers find that workers conditioned to depending on their supervisors' telling them what to do are frightened and lack confidence in their ability to solve problems and make decisions.

In addition to its effects on confidence, passive learning also undercuts the development of a particular set of higher-order cognitive skills called the "cognitive self-management," or "executive thinking," skills. These are simply the skills that we use to govern our problem-solving attempts. They include goal setting, strategic planning, checking for accurate plan execution, monitoring our progress, and evaluating and revising our plans.

We now know that those who function as independent and effective learners are people with these skills. However, as Pea (1989) observes, passive learning is disastrous for developing them. Classroom studies of reading, writing, math, and science instruction show that the executive processes for controlling thinking and learning processes are under the teacher's control, not the student's. These processes seem to get developed when the learning situation is structured to shift control from the teacher to the student, the teacher gradually removing the support that students need initially as they begin to show the ability to work autonomously.

Passive learning creates motivational and "crowd control" problems. Jordan (1987) describes a Mexican public health training program designed to improve the practice of Mayan midwives. Her analysis spotlights behaviors that American teachers constantly complain about in their students.

The teaching is organized as straight didactic material in a minilecture format. When these lectures begin, the midwives shift into what Jordan calls their "waiting-it-out" behavior: "they sit impassively, gaze far away, feet dangling, obviously tuned out. This is behavior that one might also observe in other waiting situations, such as when a bus is late or during sermons in church" (p. 3).

We see the same behaviors in American third graders. Hass (n.d.) found that students were deeply engaged in team problem-solving during their drill and practice time, but invested little attention or involvement in the teacher's instructional sessions. During three weeks of observation, the children did not adopt any of the specific strategies demonstrated by the teacher during general instruction time.

As teachers know so well, motivational problems end up as crowd control problems, illustrated by the behaviors of different groups of school children at a Metropolitan Museum display of Ice Age art and artifacts (Farnham-Diggory, 1990). Most of the school groups were moved from one exhibit to the next, pausing before each to hear a guide's or teacher's lecture. Since the children were bunched in front of an exhibit, they could not all hear the lecture, and even when they could, they lacked understanding of the time frames involved or the archaeological significance of bits of bone. Teachers had not set up the museum visit so that students became involved in what they were going to see. Groups were therefore restless and crowd control became the teacher's primary concern.

> One [exhibit] hallway was raised, and each group discovered that it could make booming noises by tramping hard over the hollow areas—booms that could never be proved to have been produced by any particular pair of feet. This seemed to provide the main entertainment of the day (p. 88).

One junior high school class behaved very differently, exhibiting a quiet intensity as they moved through the exhibit. They had packets of worksheets with questions about issues and problems that they were expected to solve at the exhibit. Some questions were factual, but most required inference and thought. The students had to figure out for themselves where and what the evidence would be concerning particular questions.

Motivational and crowd control problems with students have shown up for decades with lower-skilled workers in the forms of high turnover, absenteeism, and in extreme cases, sabotage.

Mistaken assumption #3: Learning is the strengthening of bonds between stimuli and correct responses

American education reflects a behaviorist theory of learning —a view that conceives of learning as the strengthening of bonds between stimuli and the learner's responses to those stimuli. Based on his animal experiments, the brilliant psychologist Edward Thorndike developed a new theory of learning. As Cremin (1961) observed, the theory presumed that learning was the wedding of a specific response to a specific stimulus through a physiological bond in the neural system. The stimulus [S] then regularly called forth the response [R]. The *bond* between S and R was "stamped in" by being continually rewarded; an undesired bond was extinguished through punishment or failure.

For our purposes, this psychological theory had three major effects. It led to the breakdown of complex tasks and ideas into components, subtasks, and items ("stimuli") that could be separately trained. It encouraged repetitive training ("stamping in"). And it led to a focus on the "right answer" ("successful response") and to the counting of correct responses to items and subtasks, a perspective that ended up in psychometrically elegant tests that were considered the scientific way to measure achievement.

The result was fractionation: having to learn disconnected subroutines, items, and subskills without an understanding of the larger context into which they fit and which gives them meaning. As Farnham-Diggory (1990) notes, fractionated instruction maximizes forgetting, inattention, and passivity. Since children and adults seem to acquire knowledge from active participation in complex and meaningful environments, "school programs could hardly have been better designed to prevent a child's natural learning system from operating" (p. 146).

The phrase "a child's natural learning system" goes to the heart of why the usual school programs do not meet their own learning objectives well. Human beings—even the small child—are quintessentially sense-making, problem-solving animals. "Why" is a hallmark of young children's talk. As a species, we wonder, we are curious, we want to understand. Pechman (1990) talks about the child as meaning maker. Fractionated and decontextualized instruction fails to mobilize this powerful property of human beings in the service of learning.

The point about subtasks is not that learners do not have to do simple operations. Studies of traditional apprenticeships in tailoring show that novices start with simple tasks. However, they conduct simple tasks in the context of being able to observe the master's execution of complex tailoring, which involves the integration of different subskills. Observation lets learners develop a conceptual model, or cognitive map, of what it means to be an expert tailor. This model gives learners an "advanced organizer" for their initial attempts to execute a complex skill; it provides an interpretive structure for making sense of the feedback and corrections from the master; it provides a guide to which the learner can refer during times of relatively independent practice (Collins, Brown, & Newman, 1989).

The parallel between behaviorism and Taylor's scientific management is eerie. Behaviorism conceived of the world in stimulus-response units; Taylor broke work down into precisely described and timed actions or subtasks. Today's school reformers often ascribe the problems in today's schools to Taylor's influence on the organization of work. And Taylor did powerfully affect how Americans thought about organizing activity (Callahan, 1962). However, Thorndike's work (1898) preceded Taylor's (1911), and Thorndike's influential theory of learning seems to have been a necessary precondition for schools to organize learning in ways that mirrored how companies organized work.

Mistaken assumption #4: What matters is getting the right answer

Both the transmission and the behaviorist views of learning place a premium on getting the right answer. A transmission view stresses the ability of the learner to reproduce "the Word"; a behaviorist view, the ability of the learner to generate the correct response. The end result is the same: students and teachers focus on the "right answer," jeopardizing the development of real understanding. This focus plays out in several ways.

An instructional focus on the right answer discourages instruction in problem solving. Perhaps the most serious consequence of a right answer emphasis is just that: the emphasis is on the right answer, not on how to approach the problem to be solved or on different ways to solve the same problem. A right answer focus encourages an emphasis on facts. Facts are important, but by themselves constitute an impoverished understanding of a domain; a fact-focus does not develop students' abilities to think about the domain in different ways. Cognitive analyses of a range of jobs show that being able to generate different solutions to problems that are formally the same is a hallmark of expert performance (Scribner, 1988, p. 11). Employers and college educators both complain that American high school graduates are limited in their thinking and problem-solving abilities, deficiencies that stem partly from an educational emphasis on facts and right answers.

In their observations of Chicago (U.S.A.),[1] Taipei (Taiwan), Beijing (China), and Sendai (Japan) first- and fifth-grade mathematics classes, Stigler and Stevenson (1991; Stevenson & Stigler, 1992) found that Asian teachers differ markedly from Chicago teachers. They seem to focus more on concepts, conceptual understanding, and at least in mathematics, on the notational system needed to represent concepts and their relationships. Teachers ask questions for different reasons in the United States and in Japan. In the United States, the purpose of a question is to get an answer, but Japanese teachers pose questions to stimulate thought. In fact, they consider questions to be poor if they elicit immediate answers, because this indicates that students were not challenged to think.

A common type of lesson in Asian classrooms is one that asks students to invent and evaluate different ways of solving the same problem without worrying about specifying an answer. A videotape of typical Asian classrooms (Stevenson, 1989) shows a fifth-grade teacher who started her class by showing the students a trapezoid drawn within a rectangle. She divided the class into small groups, asking each group to figure out one or more ways to determine the area of the trapezoid. She stressed that it did not matter which method they used. "You don't need to show us your calculations; just show us your method. It is your method that matters, not simply getting the correct answer." The groups came up with several different solutions, some of which were ingenious.

---

[1] The investigators sampled 40 first-grade and 40 fifth-grade classrooms from the city of Chicago and Cook County suburbs.

Lessons like these have several effects. First, they give control over problem-solving to the students, both in generating the solutions and in evaluating their mathematical validity. The teacher guides the process and insures that mathematical values are respected, but her role, in the words of an American teacher, is that of "guide on the side," not "sage on the stage."

Second, lessons such as these reproduce the actual processes in which mathematicians themselves engage—the processes of mathematical argument, discourse, and proof. By *doing* mathematics, students come to understand how mathematics got put together over the centuries, see that they can engage in the same processes, and, by virtue of participating in mathematical argument, develop a deeper understanding of mathematical concepts. Finally, because they are encouraged to generate multiple solutions to the same problem, students can regard the problem from multiple angles, thus developing a fuller understanding of its properties. They come to realize that problems can usually be solved in several ways, freeing them from an anxiety-producing hunt for the "one right way."

Students resort to veneers of accomplishment. Students respond to a focus on right answers by learning to test "right" within the school system. They figure out what answers the teacher or the test seems to want, but often at the cost of real learning. These surface achievements have been called the "veneer of accomplishment" (Lave, Smith, & Butler, 1988). Again, Jordan's (1987) analysis of a Mayan midwives' training program illuminates basic truths about the learning and testing of American students.

She found that midwives who had been through the training course saw the official health care system as powerful, in that it commanded resources and authority. They came to distinguish "good" from "not good" things to say. Specifically, they learned new ways of legitimizing themselves, new ways of presenting themselves as being in league with this powerful system, but with little impact on their daily practice. Although they could converse appropriately with supervisory medical personnel, their new knowledge was not incorporated into their behavioral repertoire. It was "verbally, but not behaviorally fixed." Jordan notes that the trainers evaluated their program by asking the midwives to reproduce definitions, lists, and abstract concepts. She observes that "if these tests measure anything at all, they measure changes in linguistic repertoire and changes in discourse skills [not changes in behavior]" (pp. 10-12).

The same behaviors show up with Hass's American third graders. He noticed that in mathematics lessons the students got much practice in problem-solving methods that they had brought into the classroom with them—methods that were not being taught and that were not supposed to be used. The children used these methods to produce right answers, which the teacher took as evidence of their having grasped the formal procedures that she was teaching them. In fact, all that had happened was the appearance of learning.

Lave, et al. (1988) cite Resnick's (1986) observations that school learners have reasonably correct calculational rules and, in the classroom, learn rules for manipulating the syntax of symbolic notation systems. However, they fail to learn the meaning of symbols and the principles by which they represent quantity. Thus wrong answers can look right and may not betray students' lack of mathematical understanding. (The attack on multiple-choice tests is targeted at the veneer problem, in that these tests fit and reinforce an emphasis on fragmented knowledge and superficially correct answers.)

We see the veneer problem in the workplace. The apparel industry study showed that for years sewing machine repair technicians had been fixing the machines—had "gotten the right answers"—in a trial-and-error, ad hoc fashion. They had not understood the principles of the technology that would have expedited and probably improved the quality of their repairs. In a sense, American corporations' new concern with quality can be seen as recognizing that veneers are no longer acceptable. To stay in business, you cannot just "look right."

Teachers do not get behind the answers. We end up with appearances of learning because, in their search for right answers, teachers often fail to check behind the answers to insure that students really grasp the principles that they want the students to master.

The evidence shows that learners carry into the learning situation conceptions and constructs that they have acquired elsewhere. (Recall Hass's students.) In other words, the teaching challenge is not to write on a clean slate. It is to confirm, disconfirm, modify, replace, and add to what is already written there.

In typical American classrooms the time devoted to a lesson on a particular topic makes it hard to bring to the surface, let alone change, the ideas and assumptions that individuals bring to the lesson. Traditional curriculum design usually is based on a conceptual analysis of the subject matter that ignores what is already in the learner's head, with the result that students make mistakes that arise from undetected ideas that they brought to the lesson. Or they can play back memorized canonical knowledge and conceptions but return to their own ideas when confronted with unfamiliar questions or nonroutine problems. As noted earlier, students in college physics courses designed for physics majors can solve "book" problems in Newtonian mechanics by rote application of formulas, but—even after instruction—revert to naive pre-Newtonian explanations of common physical situations (Raizen, 1989).

The literature on science learning gives many examples of how the learner's prior knowledge and conceptions affect new learning. As Raizen (1989) points out, both younger and older students bring to science learning their own conceptions of such natural phenomena as light, heat and temperature, electricity, or physical and chemical transformations. These ideas may be personal—i.e., constructed out of their interpretations of naive experience and coherent in their own terms—or they may come from partially understood or inappropriately applied school learning.

For example, White (1983), in diagnosing sources of students' difficulty in understanding Newtonian dynamics, found that students used varying and often inconsistent ideas in solving force and motion problems. Suppose a ball is hit and starts to roll and then is hit again from a different direction. When asked where the ball will now go, people with no physics background will usually answer that the ball will go in the direction of the last hit (diSessa, 1982). Their answers seem to neglect the momentum that the ball acquires from the first hit, probably because their everyday experiences with force and motion involve situations with friction. In these situations objects in motion slow down unless a force is constantly being applied to them, and a ball kicked for a second time is usually in a stopped state—in other words, has lost the momentum that it would still have in a frictionless world (White, 1983).

Teachers do not focus on how to use student mistakes to help them learn. In their search for right answers, teachers tend to regard student errors as "failures" rather than as opportunities to strengthen students' understanding.

Again, Asian teachers differ markedly from Chicago teachers. Stigler and Stevenson (1991; Stevenson & Stigler, 1992) found a marked difference in how American, versus Asian, teachers treated student mistakes. American teachers placed little emphasis on the constructive use of errors as a teaching technique, a practice that the researchers attribute to the strong influence of behaviorism in American education. Behaviorism requires teaching conditions that help learners make only correct responses that can be reinforced through praise.

For example, a teacher in a Japanese fifth-grade class was introducing the problem of adding fractions with unequal denominators. The problem was simple: adding 1/2 and 1/3. The teacher called on one of the students to give his answer and explain his solution. The student answered two-fifths. Pointing first to the numerators and then to the denominators, he explained that one plus one was two and three plus two was five, giving him two-fifths. Without comment the teacher asked a second student his solution. This student said that two point one plus three point one added up to five point two. When changed into a fraction, he got two-fifths. The teacher, unperturbed, asked a third student for her solution, and she answered five-sixths. She showed how she had found the common denominator, changed the fractions so that each had this denominator, and then added them.

Instead of emphasizing the correct solution and ignoring the incorrect ones, the teacher next capitalized on the errors that the first two students had made to help them and the other students confront two common misconceptions about fractions. She helped the first student test the sensibleness of his solution by asking which was larger, two-fifths or one-half? When it was acknowledged that one-half was larger, she asked whether it didn't seem strange that *adding* something to one half gave you an amount *less than* one-half? In working with the second boy, she helped him to see that he had confused decimals with fractions, but that, *given that error*, he had arrived at a sensible solution.

Mistaken assumption #5: To insure their transfer to new situations, skills and knowledge should be acquired independently of their contexts of use

This idea is often talked about as "decontextualized learning," which simply means learning in the absence of context or meaning. The rationale for decontextualized learning goes back to the presumed conditions for the transfer of learning. As Lave (1988) observes, extracting knowledge from the particulars of experience was thought to make that knowledge available for general application in all situations.

Almost three-quarters of a century earlier, John and Evelyn Dewey (1915) wrote about the learning costs of decontextualized education.

> A statement, even of facts, does not reveal the value of the fact, or the sense of its truth—of the fact that it is a fact. Where children are fed only on book knowledge, one "fact" is as good as another; they have no standards of judgment or belief. Take the child studying weights and measures; he reads in his textbook that eight quarts make a peck, but when he does examples he is apt, as every schoolteacher knows, to substitute four for eight. Evidently the statement as he read it in the book did not stand for anything that goes on outside the book, so it is a matter of accident what figure lodges in his brain, or whether any does. But the grocer's boy who has measured out pecks with a quart measure *knows*. He has made pecks; he would laugh at anybody who suggested that four quarts made a peck. What is the difference in these two cases? The schoolboy has a result without the activity of which it is the result. To the grocer's boy the statement has value and truth, for it is the obvious result of an experience—it is a *fact*.

Thus we see that it is a mistake to suppose that practical activities have only or even mainly a utilitarian value in the schoolroom. They are necessary if the pupil is to understand the facts which the teacher wishes him to learn; if his knowledge is to be real, not verbal; if his education is to furnish standards of judgment and comparison.

Resnick (1987) puts the Deweys' point in more formal language, contrasting school learning with thinking, problem solving, learning, and knowledge-using outside of school. She notes that school learning is so heavily symbol-based that connections to the things being symbolized are often lost. These symbolic activities tend to become detached from meaningful contexts, and school-like learning tends to become learning rules and saying or writing things according to rules. In nonschool situations, people's mental activities are grounded in things and situations that make sense to them.

Context turns out to be critical for understanding and thus for learning. We are back to the issue of meaning-making and sense-making discussed earlier. The importance of context lies in the meaning that it gives to learning. Brown, Collins, and Duguid (1989) argue that the constituent parts of knowledge index the world and are thus a product of the activity and situations in which they are produced.

Asian teachers rely much more heavily on context than American teachers, using both concrete objects and real-world problems more frequently (Stigler & Stevenson, 1991; Stevenson & Stigler, 1992). Sendai teachers were twice as likely and Taipei teachers five times as likely to use concrete objects as Chicago teachers to teach fifth-grade mathematics.

American teachers tend to introduce mathematical concepts and rules abstractly, only later (if ever) turning to real-world problems that involve those ideas. For example, they tend to *start* a lesson on fractions by defining *fraction* formally and naming the elements of fractional notation (denominator and numerator). Asian teachers, however, tend to introduce new mathematical ideas by first "interpreting and relating a real-world problem to the quantification that is necessary for a mathematical solution" (Stigler & Stevenson, 1991, p. 20). For example, the teacher may start the lesson by asking students to estimate how many liters of colored water are contained in a beaker. (The amount is always some part of a whole liter, such as 1 1/2 or 1 1/3 liters.) He then helps them translate their visual appreciation of "parts of" into fractional notations. The terms *fraction*, *denominator*, and *numerator* are mentioned only at the *end* of the lesson, these formal words now being connected to real-world experiences. In other words, these teachers understand that concrete experiences are not sufficient for learning—they have to be linked to formal notation and abstract concepts. However, real-world experiences provide the intuitive meaning that lets students "hook into" and "take possession of" abstract ideas.

Confusion surrounds the idea of "teaching in context." It is not about making learning "relevant," as that term came to be used in education in the 1960s. Relevance usually meant teaching subject matter directly applicable to students' lives rather than the traditional academic disciplines. This is not the same as using students' experiences to help them learn the disciplines.

Nor does teaching in context require a vocational or applied curriculum. As we just saw, Asian teachers make use of context in the form of concrete objects and real-world problems for teaching a distinctly "academic" subject (mathematics). Context is concerned with that which "connects," "makes coherent, "gives meaning," "makes interpretable" (*Oxford English Dictionary*, 1971).

And that which makes interpretable comes out of the experiences of those doing the interpreting. It is for this reason that context often gets confused with applied curricula. Context involves experience, which *comes out of* specific situations, and the presumed objective of vocational curricula is *for use in* specific situations. These are not the same thing. The fact that well-designed vocational curricula use real-world problems and objects does not mean that teaching in context is vocational teaching.

Moreover, teaching in context does not necessarily imply "multidisciplinary." Even a complex real-world object, problem, or project can be used to engage the student in a single discipline —mathematics or chemistry, for example. At the same time, any real-world problem of any complexity *lends* itself to multidisciplinary treatment. For example, a school project, discussed later in some detail, involved designing, building, and racing a solar-powered car. This project required a wide range of academic and practical disciplines, including physics and mathematics, basic solar engineering, hydraulics, electronics, drafting, model fabrication, metal working, and welding.

Contextualization can vary from using concrete objects and real-world problems in lessons to embedding learning in full-blown communities of expert practice. A community of expert practice simply refers to a social group that is organized around the performance of certain activities, where the performance is governed by shared rules, knowledge, skills, standards, procedures, technologies, and agreements about social relationships, the use of time, and incentives. Occupational groups are examples of communities of expert practice—mathematicians, cooks, doctors, geographers, electronic trouble-shooters, or poets.

Research supports the power of learning in context, as opposed to learning out of context. For example, as we saw earlier, Brazilian street vendor children solved context-embedded problems much more easily than ones without a context, the difference in correct answers being 74 percent for the former type and 37 percent for the latter type (Carraher, et al., 1985). Sticht

(1989) found that marginally literate adults in a job-related reading program gained in job-related reading twice what they gained in general reading—that is, they did better when a meaningful context was provided for the text.

Students at McMaster University School of Medicine in Ontario start immediately with clinical problems, meeting in tutorial groups with a tutor who acts as a resource person. The tutorials are organized around major biomedical problems that cannot be solved without understanding physical, biological, and behavioral principles, how to collect data, and how to evaluate evidence. The students have the responsibility of determining, with faculty help, what they need to know to solve the problem and how to get the knowledge they need.

Maastricht, a medical school in the Netherlands, uses an approach similar to McMaster's. Since the Dutch government assigns students to medical school by lottery, we can compare the effects of contextualized, problem-centered medical training with training that uses a traditional lecture approach. After seven years in school, 88 percent of Maastricht's 1974 class had received diplomas, versus 21 percent of students in other schools (Shanker, 1990).

SUMMARY

This chapter has made several arguments. One was that typical educational practices routinely and profoundly violate what we know about how people learn most effectively and the conditions under which they apply their knowledge appropriately to new situations. Passive, fragmented, and decontextualized instruction organized around generating right answers adds up to ineffective learning. In a passive learning regime, students do not gain control over their learning, let alone over what is to be learned. They are asked to learn in decontextualized and fragmented ways that destroy sense-making. The ideas that they bring to the learning situation are not made accessible to them for reexamination. Their errors are not routinely used to lead them to deeper understanding, in part by helping them see how they came to make the error. The focus on the right answer is at the cost of focusing on how to approach problems and of learning to generate different ways to solve the same problem.

These practices have to be one reason for the erratic transfer of knowledge previously acquired to new situations in which it is appropriate. Knowledge and procedures not initially well understood cannot transfer appropriately to new situations.

The second argument was that these practices permeate American education and training. We used cognitive science primarily to appraise elementary and secondary education. However, despite the rhetoric about their differences, the nation's educational and training systems do not differ particularly in their teaching and learning strategies, and the limited success that they share arises partly from shared problems in how they structure learning.

It is in corporate training, and occasionally in second-chance remedial education, that we are painfully beginning to unlearn these practices. For example, corporations as advanced in their training practices as Motorola or IBM are discovering in their own but ultimately costly way the importance of contextualized learning.

Third, without getting into a debate about whether these practices came about because schools tried to serve employers' needs, we argued that these practices were relatively consistent with how work was organized for those in lower-skill jobs, and that they did not appear to impose any particular cost on those who filled higher-skill jobs.

Finally, we argued that the pressures on U.S. industries and the resulting effects on the organization of work alter the payoffs from traditionally organized learning. Traditional education practices are now inconsistent with the skills needed in reorganized workplaces for both higher- and lower-skill jobs. Table 4 displays the relationship between characteristics of traditional learning environments and traditional workplaces described in the last chapter. The comparison in this table is more relevant to lower-skill jobs than to higher-skill ones, but some characteristics of traditionally configured lower-skill jobs infiltrate jobs that require much higher-skills.

The knowledge transfer problem mattered less in traditional workplaces because tasks were narrowly defined. Since workers were not expected to be versatile, transfer of knowledge and abilities among domains was less important.

The idea that students are passive learning vessels, acted upon by the teacher and with little control over their own learning process, closely matches the hierarchical organization of the traditional workplace. Higher-level employees are expected to receive and pass on orders; lower-level workers, to follow orders. Neither group is really expected to bring their own ideas and plans to the work. Just as this approach causes "crowd control" problems in the classroom, it leads to morale problems on the job and increases employee absenteeism and turnover.

Just as traditional learning emphasizes strengthening the bond between stimuli and correct responses, workers in the traditional workplace are expected to handle well-defined, nonambiguous situations. Workers are often trained in a limited number of responses to a limited number of possible circumstances (stimuli), and specialized support personnel and supervisors are generally expected to handle deviations from the norm. From this perspective, increasing skill can be seen as simply increasing the number of stimuli for which an individual has learned the correct responses.

Table 4.
Ineffective Learning Environments and
Traditional Workplaces: Parallels

	Characteristics of Ineffective Learning	Characteristics of Traditional Workplaces
1	Limited transfer	Narrowly defined jobs and tasks
2	Learners are passive vessels • Reduced exploration • Dependence on teacher • "Crowd control" problems	Passive order-taking in a hierarchical work organization; heavy supervision to control workers
3	Strengthening the bond between stimuli and correct response	Emphasis on specific responses to a limited number of possible problems (deviations from the expected are to be handled by specialized service personnel)
4	Emphasis on getting the right answer • No attempt to get "behind" answer • Little learning from mistakes • Little emphasis on how to think about problems	Emphasis on getting a task done rather than on improving its subsequent performance
5	Decontextualized learning	Focus on the specific task independent of its organizational context

Schools emphasize getting the right answer, with much less attention to learning from mistakes and to developing alternative ways for framing and solving problems. Correspondingly, the traditional workplace focuses on completing the task rather than understanding it and improving its subsequent performance. The traditional view of quality control matches the educational neglect of learning from mistakes. Since errors and substandard quality are repaired at the end of the production process, quality control (or error correction and process improvement) are not integrated into the core processes. Workers thus have few chances to learn from mistakes.

Finally, traditional pedagogy presumes that knowledge is only transferable if learned independently of the context in which it is subsequently used. In the traditional workplace, workers are not expected to understand much about the broader context in which they work. Context is not important when tasks are well-defined and routinized.

In sum, traditional workplaces in both service and manufacturing firms strictly limit the autonomy and responsibility accorded production workers. The separation between conception and action that characterizes these workplaces mirrors the distinction between head and hand that has played such an important role in education. Ironically, the tasks of even skilled workers are often circumscribed. Mechanics and technicians may need more skill than machine operators or lower-level clerical workers, but their jobs can still be conceived of in narrow terms. As we observed earlier, a skilled worker can be defined as someone who knows the correct responses to a larger set of stimuli. Thus what we have termed ineffective learning has been adequate for more skilled workers as well.

The link between the traditional approach to learning and the activities of professionals and managers in the traditional workplace is less obvious. If production workers are buffered from the unusual, the different, and the unexpected, it is because of the planning and responsiveness of their managers and supervisors. Some members of even the most traditionally constituted organizations cannot just passively receive orders or be involved in only a limited number of tasks. Thus a traditional education system does not serve them well.

On the other hand, where firms have been able to serve large and stable markets with slowly changing products and production processes, even supervisors and managers can operate without a deeper understanding of the processes in which they are involved. Larger traditional firms organize middle-level managers into narrow functional specializations. In other words, firms can be put together in such a way as to extend a narrow conception of jobs and tasks well above the lowest levels of the organization.

We have argued that pressures on U.S. industries are gradually driving some of them to new and innovative ways of work. In the context of these organizational innovations, production workers and many higher-level skilled and supervisory employees need a broader and more complete understanding of what they are doing. And the highest-level managers and professionals must learn to work effectively with subordinates who are no longer passive order takers—just as the jobs of teachers change when pedagogy shifts away from traditional approaches. Thus reorganized work destroys the fit between traditionally organized work and education.

What kind of education is consistent with restructured workplaces? The broad skill requirements of these workplaces and our knowledge of how individuals learn most effectively come together to imply very similar educational reform strategies.

4

EFFECTIVE LEARNING

What do more effective learning environments look like? In struggling with this problem, cognitive scientists have been drawing on a wide array of sources—nineteenth century educational thinkers; their own understanding of how the young child learns; analyses of traditional apprenticeship systems; their reflections when they themselves try to create different learning situations; and cognitive science research itself.

PRECEDENTS

Nineteenth-century educational ideas

Francis Parker was regarded by John Dewey as the founder of progressive education in the United States. In an attempt to reform the Quincy, Massachusetts, schools in 1875, Parker threw out the traditional curriculum and replaced it with educational projects and experiences meaningful to children.

John Dewey, one of the nation's great thinkers about education, built on Parker's ideas. In part, his thinking represented a response to an economic upheaval, played out a century ago: industrialization and migration from farms and small towns to the cities. As Cremin (1961) notes,

Behind the older agrarian society lay the time-honored education of the agrarian household and neighborhood, where every youngster shared in meaningful work and where the entire industrial process stood revealed to any observant child. [Dewey contended that] "... we cannot overlook the importance for educational purposes of the close and intimate acquaintance got with nature at first hand, with real things and materials, with the actual processes of their manipulation, and the knowledge of their social necessities and uses" (p. 117).

The city shut off children's chances to participate naturally in the adult world of work—in the community of practice. Dewey felt that the school had to assume the educative functions previously performed by the agrarian community itself; it had to become an "embryonic community," reflecting the life of the larger society.

His idea of the school also represented a reaction to traditional education, which he saw as isolated from reality, passive in its methods, "its educational center of gravity...[being] 'the teacher, the text-book, anywhere and everywhere you please except in the immediate instincts and activities of the child himself'" (Cremin, 1961, p. 118).

His idea of the school also fought against dualism, a philosophy that separates mind and body, spirit and matter, and that shows up in traditional distinctions made between labor and leisure, vocation and culture, the practical and the intellectual.

The curriculum at the laboratory school that Dewey founded at the University of Chicago had three principles (Farnham-Diggory, 1990):

- instruction must focus on the development of the student's mind, not on blocks of subject matter

- instruction must be integrated and project-oriented, not divided into small units (such as forty minutes of English, forty minutes of mathematics)

- through the years of schooling, the progression of the curriculum must be from practical experiences (such as planting a garden) to formal subjects (such as botany) to integrated studies (such as the place of botany in the natural sciences)

Dewey organized the curriculum around occupations: gardening, work with textiles, scholarly research, producing artistic works, manufacturing, and exploring unknown territories. The study of occupations permitted children to learn in ways that were natural and interesting to them. Occupations always involved doing something. They engaged and developed the child's motor skills and hands-on modes of learning. They required making observations, quantifying, and making predictions, thus developing the child's scientific skills. They involved other people and thus encouraged the child's social skills and interests. They required the exchange of ideas, thus providing opportunities for training in communication.

In terms of designing effective learning situations, Dewey left us certain key ideas:

- the child as the center of learning

- learning as active engagement with an environment structured for educational purposes

- the learning situation as reflecting the larger community —in other words, as a "community of practice"

- the integration of the head and hand, of mind and action, of academic and vocational

The child as spectacular learner

Analyses of the spectacular learning evidenced by young children added other clues for designing effective learning environments (Bransford, Stein, Arbitman-Smith, & Vye, 1985; Pea, 1989).

- Learning takes place in context. Children learn during the first five years in the midst of culturally meaningful, ongoing activities and receive immediate feedback on the success of their actions.

- Learning is often guided. Parents, friends, and peers not only serve as models for imitative learning, but help children learn by providing structure for and connections between their experiences. These mediators highlight information in the situation that will help children carry out a task. They let them play a role in the conduct of a whole task, such as mixing sugar and flour in the whole process of making a cake.

- Learning is useful. Learning in context and with adult guidance gives children an understanding of the role of information in problem solving. Concepts and skills are acquired as tools with a range of purposes.

- The uses of new knowledge are not only shown, but often explicitly stated—in other words, the purpose of the learning is explained.

Traditional apprenticeship learning

Another source of ideas for promoting effective learning was watching how individuals learn in traditional apprenticeships, including informal on-the-job training in American companies (Lave, in press; Jordan, 1987; Scribner & Sachs, 1990). There are striking consistencies among Dewey's ideas, the conditions for the spectacular learning of the young child, and traditional apprenticeship.

What does traditional apprenticeship look like? In her studies of Vai and Gola apprentice tailors, Lave noted that the tailoring curriculum arranges opportunities *for* practice, whereas school curricula tend to be a specification *of* practice (Lave, et al., 1988). She found that the apprentices learned tailoring through a combination of observation, coaching, and practice. Collins, Brown, and Newman (1989) note that

> In this sequence of activities, the apprentice repeatedly observes the master executing...the process [that they are trying to learn], which usually involves a number of different but interrelated subskills. The apprentice then attempts to execute the process with guidance and help from the master (coaching). A key aspect of coaching is the provision of scaffolding, which [simply means] the support, in the form of reminders and help, that the apprentice requires to approximate the execution of the entire composite of skills. Once the learner has a grasp of the target skills, the master reduces (or fades) his participation, providing only limited hints, refinements, and feedback to the learner, who practices by successively approximating smooth execution of the whole skill (p. 456).

Jordan (1987), relating her observations of apprenticing among Mayan midwives to Lave's of the Vai and Gola tailors, identifies several characteristics of traditional apprenticeship learning.

1. Apprenticeship is a way of life. Apprenticeship happens as a way of, and in the course of, daily life and may not be recognized as a teaching effort at all. In other words, there is likely to be almost no separation between the activities of daily living and the learning of "professional" skills. Much of what child apprentices do is difficult to differentiate from play, since, particularly in traditional societies, children tend to play at serious work. Our western distinction between learning as an activity in its own right and playing does not prevail. Rather, the apprentice is exposed to a certain environment, participates in sets of activities, handles (plays with) certain kinds of artifacts, and is initiated into the sphere of specialist work the same way a child is into the home environment.

2. *The work to be done is the driving force.* In apprenticeship the activities in which masters and students engage are driven by the requirements of the work to be accomplished. For example, pots need to be fired, a shawl needs to be woven, trousers need to be manufactured. The activities to which the apprentice is a witness and, by stages, a contributor are organized around work to be done, and whatever teaching or learning may happen is coincidental to that overriding concern. As a consequence, the progressive mastering of tasks by the apprentice is appreciated not so much as a step towards a distant, symbolic goal (such as a certificate), but for its immediate use value. Apprentices are not so much "practicing for the real thing" as doing useful and necessary tasks. As Lave (in press) says, the master of a tailor shop who takes on an apprentice "mainly intends to provide himself with help on a variety of errands and small sewing tasks."

3. *There is a temporal ordering of skill acquisition.* Apprentices start with skills that are relatively easy and where mistakes are least costly. For example, the young tailor apprentice's first assignments are sewing garments from pieces someone else has cut, not constructing it from start to finish. Only when the individual production processes are mastered is the entire production sequence put together. Similarly, among Zinacanteco

Indian weavers, major chunks of the garment construction process (e.g., dyeing, spinning, weaving, sewing) are learned in an order which reflects economic concerns, i.e., the relative cost of novice errors, rather than the standard order of production.

The concept of working from the sidelines of a complex task to its center stands in contrast to the ways that knowledge is usually transferred in formal schooling. In a formal classroom there is usually a (chrono)logically ordered sequence of things to be learned. The components are treated as equal in importance to one another, and it is assumed that they have to be acquired in a linear way—in other words, one after the other, rather than in "bundles."

4. *Traditional apprenticeship learning focuses on bodily performance and embodied knowledge.* When lectures are used to convey knowledge, the focus is on verbal and abstract knowledge. However, apprenticeship learning is the acquisition of bodily skills. It involves the ability to do rather than the ability to talk about something. Indeed, it may be impossible to elicit from people operating in this mode what they know how to do. The master is less likely to talk than to guide the hands, producing truly embodied knowledge. In the apprenticeship mode, acquisition of bodily skills is primary, while the verbalization of general principles is secondary, ill developed, and not well rehearsed.

5. *Standards of performance and evaluation of competence are implicit.* What constitutes expert execution of a task is obvious and observable in the master's performance. Judgments about the learner's competence emerge naturally and continuously in the context of the work being accomplished rather than occurring as a specially marked event, such as a test. The success or failure of a task that has been performed is obvious and needs no commentary. To a large extent, the person who judges the apprentice's performance is the apprentice himself or

herself rather than the expert. The apprentice, having observed the work sequence many times, knows what remains to be learned. Moving on to the acquisition of the next skill may be up to the apprentice and largely under her or his own control rather than the master's. In other words, the apprentice tends to "own the problem" of moving on to learn the next skill.

6. *Teachers and teaching are largely invisible.* In apprenticeship learning—and during informal on-the-job training in modern American workplaces—it looks as though little teaching is going on. Teaching does not occur as an identifiable activity, and whatever instruction the apprentice receives originates, not from a teacher doing teaching, but from a weaver/tailor/stockroom worker doing his or her work that the apprentice observes.

Summary. An apprenticeship situation consists of a community of experts and novices, analogous to Dewey's agrarian community. Apprenticing is a process of being inducted into the community of expert practice, whether the practice is that of tailoring, weaving, or farming. Critical to this learning situation is that the "teacher" continuously engages in and is a master at the practice being learned. His or her performances constitute the standards of performance for the apprentice.

Clearly, traditional apprenticeships are not entirely transferable to a modern society. For example, practices such as tailoring or weaving are physically observable to the novice, and embodied knowledge—the knowledge of the hand—is important. However, many modern practices, whether in mathematics, law, or computer-based machining, are only partly visible. Embodied knowledge is less important.

At the same time, traditional apprenticeships show what contextualized, effective learning looks like. Given the images of traditional apprenticeships, cognitive scientists have been able to invent analogues appropriate for learning less-visible practices.

Actual trials

A final source of knowledge for crafting effective learning situations is cognitive scientists' own efforts to design them. These efforts span a number of subjects—for example, mathematics (e.g., Schoenfeld, 1985), physics (White, 1983, 1984), reading (Palincsar & Brown, 1984, 1989), writing (Scardamalia & Bereiter, 1985), and interior design (Stasz, McArthur, Lewis, & Ramsey, 1990).

Schoenfeld's (1988) design efforts in mathematics are representative of these efforts. He first identified the learning objectives that he had for his students. He wanted them

- to understand that a major part of the mathematical enterprise consists of looking for and seeing connections, not simply getting answers. From this perspective, solving a given problem does not represent the end of the mathematical enterprise, but a beginning; further steps include finding alternative solutions to the problem, generalizing the solution, relating it to other mathematics, and so on.

- to see that mathematics is something that they can generate by themselves rather than a fixed body of facts and procedures developed by others that must be memorized.

- to understand that both conjecture and proof are legitimate and related parts of the mathematical enterprise, and that the interplay of the two results in the development of one's own mathematical understandings.

To attain these objectives, he had to create a learning environment different from the standard mathematics class. Echoing traditional apprenticeships and Dewey's occupational focus, he tried to create a "community of mathematical practice," the learning objective being to induct students into the community of mathematicians.

> I try to create what might be called a *microcosm of mathematical practice*...The courses are a partially managed environment: I have a sense of what I want to achieve in them and of what problems will serve as fertile sources of ideas and explorations...It is essential for me to help the students find fertile grounds for mathematical exploration...But then it is equally essential for me gradually to remove myself from the process, moving to the side and prompting the group to resolve issues by itself. I remain engaged as a member of the community, making sure that the appropriate mathematical values are respected (Are we really sure? Is there a counterexample?). I refrain, however, from pronouncing what is right and what is wrong; I pose the issues and leave it (for as long as possible) for the class to resolve them...At their own level the students are mathematicians, engaged in the practice of mathematical sense-making. They do mathematics, with the same sense of engagement and involvement. The difference is that the boundaries of understanding that they challenge are the boundaries of their own understanding, rather than those of the mathematical community at large (pp. 12-13).

Schoenfeld sees similarities between his research work with professional mathematicians and the activities of students in his mathematics class, suggesting that he has managed to create a learning environment that reproduces the environment of expert practice.

- We work on substantial and meaningful problems. The few "skill development" exercises in which we engage in either environment are chosen because we feel we need the skills.

- There is a sense of commitment to the enterprise, and to the sense of values shared by the community.

- It's fun. There is pleasure in the involvement, in the progress being made, and in the results achieved (p. 14).

When we compare Schoenfeld's practices to those that usually prevail in classrooms, we start to see how to design our way out of ineffective learning situations. For example, we know that passive learning reduces or removes chances for exploration, discovery, and invention. In selecting mathematics problems for the class, Schoenfeld looks for ones that can "serve as fertile sources of ideas and explorations." We know passive learning places control over learning in the teacher's, not the learner's, hands. Schoenfeld gradually removes himself from the process and prompts the group to resolve issues by itself. His major role is to insure that the rules that govern the conduct of mathematics are respected and to pose questions that challenge the group.

We know that a focus on getting the right answer encourages veneers of accomplishment in learners. Schoenfeld sees the point of class, not as getting right answers, but as opportunities for mathematical sense-making. The difference between mathematicians doing mathematics and these students is "that the boundaries of understanding that they challenge are the boundaries of their own understanding, rather than those of the mathematical community at large." This engagement with the real stuff of mathematics is antithetical to sounding and testing "right" within the school system.[1]

Most telling is an incident in Schoenfeld's class that shows the positive motivational effects of engaged and debated learning.

> The students work in small groups for perhaps half the class. Then we convene as a whole to discuss those problems ... One day toward the end of the term I had an unavoidable conflict during the first part of class. I asked a colleague to hand out my problem set; the students could work by themselves for a while, and I'd join them when I could. Unfortunately, I was detained, and only managed to get free after class was over. I ran to the room where the class met, arriving fifteen minutes after

---

[1]Schools in the State of Vermont seem to be creating environments that produce deep, not superficial, learning.

In Mrs. Rainey's eighth-grade algebra class at Shelburne Middle School in Shelburne, Ryan Galt, 13, swiftly explained with a lighted overhead projector how he got the solution to a problem. He calculated madly, his pencil flying through numbers as he talked.

Suddenly out of the darkened classroom came the kind of sheer admiration usually reserved for a wheeling, over-the-head basketball jam by the Chicago Bulls guard Michael Jordan: "Jeez, that's sweet," cried Casey Recupero. He had had the same correct answer as Ryan, he explained, but was delighted by the other student's elegant methodology.

As the class ended, clusters of students compared their approaches to the problem with the passionate ardor that teachers everywhere dream of inspiring. "I had an interesting way of doing it, but I messed up," one student said. "That's because you did this here," his classmate said, pointing out an error (DeWitt, 1991).

class should have ended. All the students were still there, still in small groups, arguing over the problems (pp. 12-13).[2]

COGNITIVE APPRENTICESHIP MODELS

These precedents—nineteenth century innovations; analyses of the spectacular learning of the young child; analyses of traditional apprenticeships; actual attempts by cognitive scientists to create different kinds of learning environments; and cognitive science research itself—add up to a solid foundation for designing effective learning environments. Collins, Brown, and Newman (1989) have proposed what they believe to be key elements of these environments, calling the emergent model "cognitive apprenticeship."

The cognitive apprenticeship model modifies traditional apprenticeship to teach symbolically-based, and therefore less observable, activities such as reading, writing, and mathematics. The term *cognitive* should not be read to mean "academic." The model ignores our usual distinctions between academic and vocational education, in that its objective is to induct the novice into communities of expert practice, whether the practice is what the rest of us might call academic—for example, mathematics—or

---

[2]As the State of Vermont has moved to portfolio assessment, classrooms are looking more and more like Schoenfeld's and finding the same motivational effects. Joan Simmons, an eighth-grade English teacher, has found that "As a teacher, you have to be willing to give up control, give up being a talking head. But if you do, after a little confusion, the rewards are fantastic. Discipline problems go out the window and the kids are engaged" (DeWitt, 1991).

vocational—for example, interior design.[3] In other words, the model presumes that learning is learning, however the rest of us may choose to label the domain being studied.

In fact, chapter 2 showed that in a restructuring American economy, many vocational domains today involve substantial amounts of symbolic activity. Several occupations that previously depended primarily on the skilled hand and the skilled eye now also require facility with symbolic material. For example, in traditional machining, responsibility for part dimensions and tolerances, metal properties, and tool use is literally in the hands of the machinists, whose knowledge of part geometry, metallurgy, output requirements, and tool functioning is extensive. Computerized numerical control (CNC) machines radically alter the process by replacing manual setup and control with setup by symbolic command. Whereas the machinist working on a traditional machine reads an engineer's blueprint and then manually adjusts dials and levers to set up a particular operation, a machinist on the CNC machine reads the blueprint and then creates commands in a programming language to govern the machine's operations (Martin, Scribner, & Beach, 1990).

In the textile industry, textile machines used to be mechanically based. Workers could visually observe how they operated, and working around them gave operators a sense of how to repair them. The additional training needed to become a fixer was acquired on the job with little or no formal instruction. This situation has now changed. Most machines now have microprocessors and other electronic components. Since important machine components are not visually observable, operating the

---

[3]The subtitle of the authors' original paper on cognitive apprenticeship is revealing in this respect, "teaching the craft of reading, writing, and mathematics." The subjects might be seen as academic, but their practice is defined as a craft.

machines does not provide much sense of what it takes to repair and maintain them. To understand, diagnose, and fix the new machines, technicians now have to be able to represent their structures and processes symbolically in their heads. To do this, they have to be able to follow complicated manuals, diagrams, and updates provided by the manufacturers. Literacy requirements have accordingly shot up.

Collins, Brown, and Newman (1989) argue that the most important difference between formal schooling and apprenticeship is that, in schooling, skills and knowledge are abstracted from their uses in the world; in apprenticeship, they are continually used by skilled practitioners and are instrumental to accomplishing meaningful tasks. In other words, "apprenticeship embeds the learning of skills and knowledge in their social and functional context" (p. 454).

Thus their focus is on learning through guided experience, but emphasizing cognitive skills and processes rather than the physical ones that characterize traditional apprenticeship. In traditional apprenticeships, the target skills, such as expert tailoring, are visually observable—they are external in the sense that they can literally be seen and are available to students and teachers for "observation, comment, refinement, and correction." (Collins, Brown, & Newman, 1989, p. 457) Externalized skills, such as the assembly of pieces into a shirt, have a fairly transparent relationship to concrete products. This ability to see the relevant skills, procedures, and resulting products helps the student build a conceptual model of the complex target skill—to envision his or her ultimate performance goal. And the relatively transparent relationship, at all stages of production, between process and product facilitates the learner's recognition and diagnosis of errors, upon which the early development of self-correction skills depends.

In contrast, applying apprenticeship methods to skills that are not particularly visually observable—in other words, to largely cognitive skills—means that ways have to be found to externalize processes

> that are usually carried out internally...As most subjects are taught and learned in school, teachers cannot make fine adjustments in students' application of skill and knowledge to problems and tasks, because they have no access to the relevant cognitive processes. By the same token, students do not usually have access to the cognitive problem-solving processes of instructors as a basis for learning through observation and mimicry (Collins, Brown, & Newman, 1989, pp. 4-5).

Defining characteristics of cognitive apprenticeship

Keeping this challenge in mind and analyzing exemplary instructional programs in reading, writing, and mathematics, Collins, Brown, and Newman (1989) identified characteristics of ideal learning environments. Their model has four building blocks: content, methods, sequence, and sociology. It is these pieces *working together* that define an effective learning situation.

CONTENT

Target knowledge for an ideal learning environment includes domain-specific conceptual, factual, and procedural knowledge and three types of strategic knowledge. Schools usually focus only on domain-specific content. However, strategic content is needed to operate effectively with domain-particular knowledge.

- **Domain Knowledge**: the conceptual and factual knowledge and procedures associated with a particular subject—e.g., geography, repairing textile machinery, comparative literature, physics, accounting, architecture, radiology, contract law.

- **Tricks of the Trade**: referred to more formally as heuristic strategies, these are problem-solving strategies that experts have picked up with experience. They do not always work, but when they do, they are quite helpful.

- **Cognitive Management Strategies**: these govern the process of carrying out a task and are also known as executive thinking skills, or metacognitive skills. They include goal setting, strategic planning, checking for accurate plan execution, goal-progress monitoring, plan evaluation, and plan revision.

- **Learning Strategies**: these are strategies for learning any of the kinds of content described above. Knowledge about how to learn includes general strategies for exploring a new domain. It also includes strategies for getting more knowledge in an area already partially understood and reconfiguring knowledge already possessed.

METHODS

Teaching methods should be designed to give students the chance to observe, engage in, invent, or discover expert strategies in context.

- **Modeling**: for students to model expert performance, the learning situation must include an expert performing a task so that students can observe and build a conceptual model of the processes that are required.[4]

- **Coaching**: observing students as they carry out a task and offering hints, support, feedback, modeling, reminders, and new tasks to bring their performances closer to expert performance.

- **Scaffolding and Fading**: scaffolding refers to the supports that a teacher provides to help a student carry out a task. Supports can take the form of either suggestions or help or actual physical supports, such as the short skis used to teach downhill skiing. Fading is the gradual removal of supports

---

[4]In cognitive domains, this requires the externalization of usually internal cognitive processes and activities. For example, an expert's exercise of cognitive self-management skills is normally a silent and unobservable activity. In cognitive apprenticeship situations, the expert (teacher) might model the reading process by reading aloud in one voice and verbalizing her/his thought processes in another.

until students are on their own. Fading is critical to autonomous and independent functioning.

- **Articulation**: any method that gets students to articulate their knowledge, reasoning, or problem-solving processes in a domain. It makes visible otherwise invisible cognitive process-es. It also makes explicit assumptions that students bring to the learning situation.

- **Reflection**: any technique that allows students to compare their own problem-solving processes with those of an expert, another student, or ultimately an internal cognitive model of expertise.

- **Exploration**: any device that pushes students into a mode of problem solving on their own. Forcing them to explore is critical if they are to learn how to frame questions or problems that are interesting and that they can solve. This part of the model provides the opportunities for the experiential feedback that is so key to learning.

SEQUENCING

Learning should be staged so that the learner builds the
multiple skills required in expert performance and dis-
covers the conditions in which they can be generalized.

- **Increasing Complexity**: sequencing tasks and task environ-ments to require more and more of the skills and concepts necessary for expert performance.

- **Increasing Diversity**: constructing tasks so that they require a wider and wider variety of strategies or skills. This strategy helps students learn to distinguish the conditions under which they do (and do not) apply. (This principle is key to students seeing the possibilities for and the limits of transfer.)

- **Global before Local Skills**: staging the learning so that students first develop a sense of the overall terrain before attending to its details. Having a mental image of the overall activity helps students make sense of the subactivity that they are carrying out. It also acts as a guide for the learner's performance.

SOCIOLOGY

The learning environment should reproduce the technological, social, chronological, and motivational characteristics of the real-world situations in which what is being learned will be used.

- **Situated (Contextualized) Learning**: students carrying out tasks and solving problems in a way that reflects the nature of such tasks in the real world. For example, reading and writing instruction might be situated in the context of an electronic message system that students use to send each other questions and advice.

- **Community of Expert Practice**: a learning environment where participants actively communicate about and engage in the skills evidenced by experts. In other words, the learning situation needs to include experts and learners; experts performing tasks; and learners being drawn into the community of expert practice by watching experts, working with experts to solve problems and carry out tasks, and coming to assume autonomous control over problems and tasks.

- **Intrinsically Motivated Learning**: the incentives that govern the learning situation. Intrinsic motivation arises when students are engaged with interesting, or at least coherent, goals rather than for some extrinsic reason, such as pleasing the teacher.

- **Cooperative Learning**: students working together to solve problems and carry out tasks. Learning through cooperative problem solving is both a powerful intrinsic motivator and a way to extend learning resources. For example, in computer clubs, nonexperts are able to use each other as scaffolding for increasing their command of computers. By pooling their fragments of knowledge they are able to bootstrap themselves toward expertise (Levin, 1982).

- **Competitive Learning**: giving students the same task to carry out and then comparing their performances to focus their attention on strengths and weaknesses. Learning in today's classrooms is competitively, and usually destructively, structured. For competition to be constructive, comparisons should be made, not on the products of student problem solving, but on the processes that generate the products. The learning objectives for students should be defined not as making no errors but as learning to spot errors and using an understanding of them to improve. Combining cooperative and competitive learning can mitigate the destructive aspects of competition: for example, students might work together in teams to compete with other teams, thus letting them use team members as scaffolding and comparisons of team performances to focus attention on better ways to carry out a task.

The *content* building block includes knowledge and procedures specific to a domain, which is simply a subject, such as Russian literature, photography, structural engineering, cooking, economics, dancing, or statistics. The content block also includes strategies for effectively using and expanding one's grasp of domain-particular knowledge and procedures. These strategies correspond roughly to what are called the higher-order thinking skills, taught, in the context of, not separate from particular content.

The *methods* building block describes the work relationship of teacher and students—their roles and responsibilities. It also identifies ways of making visible and accessible to teacher and students the reasoning, knowledge, and strategies that students bring to their problem solving.

The third building block focuses on the *sequencing* of learning. It talks about deepening knowledge—increasing the student's expertise. It talks about broadening knowledge—understanding more about where and how the knowledge and skills can be appropriately used. It talks about how to stage the initial acquisition of knowledge—finding ways to let the student see the whole before trying to develop the subskills implicated in producing the whole. For example, being able to watch an expert tailor construct a garment gives students mental representations, or cognitive maps, of their ultimate goal. They can then use that map as an organizer for their early attempts to acquire the subskills involved in the expert performance.

The final building block discusses the *sociology* of the learning situation, i.e., the importance of reproducing the characteristics of the real-world situations in which what is being learned will be

used. Among these characteristics are the technology, the social
relationships and incentives, and the time frames that govern real-
world tasks. For example, the learning situation should set up
both cooperative and competitive incentives for learning. It
should teach content in the context of real-world problems.

Examples of cognitive apprenticeship

Any statement of principles is abstract, and the number of
principles involved in cognitive apprenticeship seems daunting.
However, we find instances of such apprenticeships not just in the
annals of cognitive scientists but also in real-world high school
courses and projects designed by real-world high school teachers.

Redesigning the American Constitution. Salomon (1990)
describes a project for studying the American Constitution.
Recognizing that studying constitutions is not very exciting for
eighth graders, the designers first thought about structuring the
project so that the students could create a computer database that
they could use to sort information, reconstruct it into newly
invented categories, and so forth. However, they immediately
asked themselves: Why would students want to do this? They
realized that individuals rarely classify novel information and cross-
tabulate it without having a reason for doing so. "And how does
one classify legal clauses, according to what criteria, in the absence
of a clear purpose" (p. 8)?

Salomon and his colleagues were struggling with the issue of
meaning for the students, the problem addressed by authentic
situated learning.

They created a purpose by asking students to take the
positions of different stakeholders—the federalists, the loyalists,
representatives from the different colonies (New York, Penn-
sylvania, Virginia, etc.), plantation owners. Working in teams of
three, the students treated the Constitution as a draft, proposing

changes in it according to their stakeholder perspectives. This gave them a reason and a framework for dealing with the Constitution in database form, and they were encouraged to reclassify its clauses, compare them, and draw out the implications for their political positions. They then formulated proposed changes in the Constitution to be introduced in subsequent interteam debates.

In other words, the Constitution is not treated as The Word, but as a document that was originally built out of dynamic political forces and that students can rebuild in the same spirit.

The project culminated in a Constitutional Convention, where the teams, under the guidance of George Washington (the teacher), debated the changes that they wanted adopted. Three students became clerks of the Convention to count votes and announce decisions, and other students served as an audience. Creating a position to take to the Convention generated opportunities for students to develop their knowledge, reasoning, and problem solving. It also allowed them to reflect on their efforts by letting each student compare his/her own problem-solving processes with those of other students in the team. The Constitutional Convention created more opportunities for articulation and reflection, and, because it had important elements of competition and public comparison, it helped the teams to focus their attention on the strengths and weaknesses of their performances.

Building and racing a solar-powered car. Students from Conval High School in Peterborough, New Hampshire, built and raced a solar-powered car (National Council on Vocational Education, 1990). This applied science project evidences all four blocks of the cognitive apprenticeship model.

The project extended over nine months, an unusually long time frame for a school, but a realistic one for real-world tasks. It culminated in the team's competition in a 234-mile, five-day race from Montpelier, Vermont, to Boston, a goal that created both cooperative and competitive incentives.

The project required the students to acquire and use a wide variety of skills spanning many academic and practical disciplines, including physics and mathematics, basic solar engineering, hydraulics, electronics, drafting, model fabrication, metal working, and welding. Ten models were built and tested before the students finally decided on a production design. This decision process required them to articulate and reflect on the strengths and weaknesses of each model.

The students quickly learned the necessity for other skills as well. They had to acquire the business skills necessary to manage some grant funds. They also had to learn the English, journalism, and graphics skills needed for a public relations effort about the project. Perhaps most surprising to the students, they had to acquire the leadership, management, and interpersonal relations skills necessary to construct a rational division of labor to keep the project moving forward. Among the more significant outcomes of the management process was a negotiated decision to build the car for racing safety at the sacrifice of speed, a decision that forced students to articulate their positions, to reflect on the merits of those positions, and to cooperate with each other.

William Bigelow, their instructor, had four educational goals: (1) the project should control curriculum in a way that enabled students to see worthwhile connections between their work and real environmental and economic problems; (2) the students should become managers of their own learning—in other words, they should learn what they needed to know to accomplish specific goals through team decision-making; (3) the project should integrate study across the curriculum—for example, the project's success depended as much on a solid PR effort involving journalism skills as on understanding the physics of photovoltaics; and (4) the students should learn the necessity of building bridges to critical local resources to acquire the technical support and financial assistance required.

Reciprocal teaching to strengthen reading comprehension. Palincsar and Brown (1984) developed reciprocal teaching to increase students' reading comprehension, especially that of poor readers. Collins, Brown, and Holum (1991) observe that reciprocal teaching embodies several features of cognitive apprenticeship. The method involves modeling and coaching students in four strategic skills: formulating questions based on the text, summarizing the text, making predictions about what will come next, and clarifying difficulties with the text. Both teacher and students first read a paragraph silently. Whoever is playing the role of teacher formulates a question based on the paragraph, constructs a summary, and makes a prediction or clarification. The teacher initially models the process and then turns the role of teacher over to the students, coaching them extensively at first on how to construct good questions and summaries and critiquing their efforts. The teacher ultimately fades into the role of monitor, providing occasional hints or feedback.

Poor readers improved their reading comprehension scores from 15 to 85 percent accuracy after twenty training sessions. Six months later they were still at 60 percent, recovering to 85 percent with one session.

Collins, Brown, and Holum (1991) attribute the success to several factors. First, the method engages the students in activities that help them form a new conceptual model of the task of reading. They are reading to understand what they are reading and developing the critical ability to read to learn. The second factor seems to be that the teacher models expert strategies in a shared-problem context. Students can compare their own questions or summaries with the questions or summaries generated by the group. They can reflect on any differences, trying to understand what causes them. The third factor seems to be the provision of scaffolding. Finally, students assume the dual roles of producer and critic. They not only must produce good questions and summaries but also learn to appraise those of others. By becoming critics as well as producers, students are forced to articulate their knowledge about what makes a good question, prediction, or summary. This knowledge then becomes available for use in their own summaries and questions. Moreover, once articulated, this knowledge is freed from its contextual binding and becomes available for use in different contexts.

Designing the six-room interior of an historic Victorian house. Stasz et al. (1990) describe a high school interior design class where students had six weeks to complete a contemporary interior design for an historic Victorian house. They had to research the original house and the design tradition, draw the house, draft the floor plan, select furnishings and coordinate colors, and prepare boards to display the proposed design. Most of the students worked in teams of four to six people, but some worked individually.

To help students learn from errors, the teacher frequently provided coaching and support. However, in general, she backed away from active coaching. She tried to structure the project so that it naturally produced opportunities for students to learn skills such as "monitoring as you go."

She worked to foster what Collins, Brown, and Newman (1989) call exploration. Although some aspects of the interior design project were constrained, she deliberately under-constrained the task to encourage students to create their own problems and solutions. She pushed students to the boldness and risk-taking associated with exploration.

Bob shows Ms. Adams a wallpaper sample in beige. Ms. Adams looks at it and asks Bob if he can't "come up with something less safe." Bob, looking puzzled, asks what is wrong with beige. Ms. Adams turns the question around, but Bob cannot respond. She explains that beige is not a design challenge: "There is nothing to do with it. You can't make a mistake with it." She then told the research team: "If I had spoon-fed the kids, it would have defeated the whole purpose of the project; they would have never shifted gears. They were frustrated when they did not get the answer, but they learned that it's okay for them to have an opinion as long as it's backed by a rationale. Liking something is not enough" (p. 26).

In the final analysis: How effective is cognitive apprenticeship?

We do not yet know whether cognitive apprenticeship is effective in routine as opposed to hothouse learning situations. However, the ideas are unusually well grounded and small studies, like the ones of Palincsar and Brown's reciprocal teaching, suggest the potential for spectacular improvements in learning.

Cognitive apprenticeship strategies build on traditional apprenticeship, a tested, crosscultural strategy for effectively acquiring visually observable skills. They build on and incorporate the ideas and findings of a community of serious thinkers and researchers, from John Dewey to today's cognitive scientists.

However, learning situations that reflect cognitive apprenticeship principles are not thick on the ground. Extending them requires dealing with institutional, curricular, pedagogic, evaluation, and professional training issues. The model itself will change as we gain experience with it in the bruising real world of teaching and learning.

5

POLICY
RECOMMENDATIONS AND
IMPLICATIONS

This book has argued that, during most of the postwar era, U.S. business was built on and prospered with a mass production system. Several economic factors are now combining to gradually undermine the strengths of this system. Flexibility, fast response to market shifts, and continuous innovation are becoming increasingly key to effective competition.

These changes carry implications for the skill requirements of different levels of workers and thus for our education and training system. They alter what workers at all skill levels need to know, how they need to use what they know, and when they need to learn it.

The learning practices of our schools were relatively consistent with how work was organized during the mass production era in the U.S. economy. However, the pressures on U.S. industries and their effects on the organization of work are altering the payoffs of traditionally organized learning, rendering these traditional practices inconsistent with the skills required in restructured workplaces.

We delineated an alternative organization of learning that promises to markedly increase the effectiveness of students' learning time, to involve the less motivated more deeply and productively in learning, and that fits the skills required in their contexts of use.

What do these ideas imply for educational policy? How do they interface with educational reform ideas that are already on the table?

WHAT DO WE RECOMMEND?

Change the mission of K-12 schools to position all students for middle- and high-skill jobs

This recommendation rests on assumptions about the long-term trend in the economy's skill requirements and wages for lower-skill work. We read the evidence as an uneven and gradual trend toward both the elimination and the restructuring of lower-skill work, leaving a slowly increasing proportion of jobs that require the skills and knowledge traditionally associated with middle- and high-skill work.[1]

However the data are interpreted on the skill direction of the U.S. economy, no one disputes that the economy has been shedding low-skill jobs that pay middle-level wages. Increasingly, only middle-skill and high-skill jobs pay wages that allow family formation and maintenance.[2]

---

[1]Examples of middle-skill jobs include travel agents, maintenance and repair technicians, and health technicians. High-skill jobs include professional and managerial jobs, such as lawyer, engineer, or corporate executive.

[2]Most students who leave school without this preparation will not be able to survive economically except in any one or some combination of four ways: work in low-skill jobs whose low wages mean that even minor unanticipated expenses become financial crises; engage in illegal activities; receive government assistance of some type; or live off of someone else's earnings.

It is true that low-skill jobs, such as food service jobs or simple clerical jobs, still exist in abundance, and it is not easy to envision how many of these could be restructured to require middle-level skills that generate moderate wages. However, the requirements of the economy must be distinguished from educational objectives for individuals. The skills that jobs require are not necessarily those that individuals require. If our educational objectives include giving individuals economic options, they need the education increasingly required across jobs of many types, if not by all types of jobs. Discrimination—whether based on race, ethnicity, gender, age, or handicap—is alive and well in labor markets. However, the power of discrimination to trap individuals in bad jobs, regardless of their capabilities, has waned over the last quarter century. Human capital is gradually becoming more important in determining an individual's economic opportunities.

The educational implications of these economic realities are stark, fundamental, and unavoidable. All students, not just some, now need the knowledge and skills required for middle- and high-skill jobs, whether or not they start their work careers in jobs of this sort. Since most of these jobs will require post-K-12 training, the K-12 responsibility is to insure that high school graduates exit with the types and levels of skills and knowledge needed to complete additional training, whether in postsecondary programs or employer-sponsored training.

The need to develop relatively high levels of knowledge and skills in all K-12 students means that the mission of our schools has to change. If our schools have a mission at all—and for some even that is problematic (Hill, Foster, & Gendler, 1990)—it is primarily an academic mission for a subset of students. Historically, K-12 has been organized around further education, not around serious, coherent preparation for work which may in fact require further education. K-12 schools generally do not see the economic preparation of their students as their responsibility, any gestures in this direction being isolated in vocational education programs that are often of poor quality or, at best, in career magnet schools.[3] Even the general track in schools, now broadly acknowledged as an educational wasteland, was designed as a more accessible—and ultimately debased—academic track, not as a high-quality vocational track that fused academic and vocational content and skills.

Thus, non-baccalaureate-bound students, even those who ultimately complete a community college program, have been less prepared than carried along, or warehoused. The costs of this organization of our schools were less obvious when jobs that did not require serious coherent preparation were more prevalent and some share of these jobs paid middle-level wages. However, changes in the U.S. economy have increased the costs of an educational system that is missing the middle—in other words, serious, coherent preparation for the middle-skill jobs that are replacing lower-skill jobs. The mismatch between the implicit mission of most high schools and the skill implications of economic changes has hurt all non-baccalaureate-bound youth. It has been devastating for poor children, whose meager resources make them most dependent on the schools for opportunity.

---

[3]In 1984 the Gallup Poll asked public school teachers and the general public to rate the importance of eight alternative goals of education on a scale of one to ten. Of these goals, the greatest differences emerged for the economic objectives of education. Fifty-six percent of the public and 20 percent of the teachers gave the highest rating to the goal, "To develop an understanding about different kinds of jobs and careers, including their requirements and rewards." Similarly, 46 percent of the public, but only 6 percent of the teachers, gave the highest rating to the goal, "To help students get good/high-paying jobs" (*Phi Delta Kappan*, 1985).

Dissolve the dualism that perpetuates the deep division between vocational education and academic education

The mismatch between the focus of our K-12 schools and serious, coherent economic preparation for our students is deeply rooted in the dualism between culture and vocation, head and hand, abstract and concrete, theoretical and applied. In the schools, this dualism manifests itself in decontextualized academics and academically debased vocational education. Cremin (1961) points out that John Dewey discussed this dualism almost a century ago.

> For centuries culture had meant the possession of certain kinds of knowledge marking the knower as a member of a superior social group. From the time of the Greeks it had been associated with wealth as opposed to poverty, with leisure as opposed to labor, with theory as opposed to practice. And in the school curriculum it had come to imply an emphasis on certain literary and historical studies, the knowledge of particular classical works, and the mastery of particular foreign languages. For Dewey the notion of culture inevitably emphasized the differences among classes rather than their commonalities, exclusiveness rather than association. Moreover, while it was thoroughly utilitarian for some social groups—statesmen, professionals, intellectuals—it was equally irrelevant for others. On two counts, then—that of exclusiveness and that of inequity—the historic view of culture was blatantly aristocratic (p. 124).

This view of "culture" is alive and well in the U.S. educational reform movement. President Bush's education strategy, *America 2000* (1991), de facto conceives of K-12 as an academic preparation system (the five core subjects of English, mathematics, science, history, and geography). In a sense, it is simply a more choice-oriented version of *A Nation at Risk* (1983), which was a call for a return to higher academic standards and requirements. A view of education as supporting work enters the strategy, but entirely in the context of training adults and experienced workers.

The organization of work in the United States for much of this century also has made it difficult for teachers who might want to bridge the gap between the academic and the vocational. How could they put together desires to develop their students' minds with preparing them for jobs that were not high skill? Preparing students for college did not present a conflict for them. As Dewey observed, academics *were* utilitarian for the baccalaureate-bound who would subsequently enter higher-skill jobs. Foreign languages and history *were* useful for those contemplating foreign service; mathematics *was* useful to those planning to become engineers or scientists.

However, given how the U.S. economy was organized, educating the non-baccalaureate-bound for the economy meant educating the hand, not the head. It meant teaching specific and limiting rather than general principles, and socializing the individual for hierarchical and restrictive economic institutions. Recall the observation that working the line at G.M. was like being paid to flunk high school for the rest of your life (see p. 50). Teachers who cared about the development of their students' potential could not see how to reconcile this objective with economic futures like the G.M. assembly line. In a sense, employers who are today concerned about young people's knowledge and skills are reaping the whirlwind that their predecessors helped to sow.

Parental attitudes still support the dualism. Parents, poor and rich alike, have clearly understood the society's message: college —and the high school academic track that gets you there—is the only destination that gives their children a shot at an economically viable future. In the absence of a national system organized around preparing students for middle- and higher-skill jobs, anything other than the academic track and college amounts to no preparation, which at best translates into low-skill jobs.

Thus parents resist any reform that sounds as though it might preclude college for their children.[4] They are willing to settle for the general track, a virtual wasteland, because it purports to give weaker students "academic," albeit applied academic, training. "Vocational," "workplace," and "applied" are all heard as warning bells.

As Dewey observed, the dualism between head and hand gains some of its staying power because it is used to create and mark privilege. For example, when courts have ruled that a state must move in the direction of equalizing its educational expenditures across its children, we see immediate attempts by the more privileged to buy advantage for their children by setting up private foundations to fund extra opportunities in their children's schools.

In other words, although our educational system provides opportunity to some extent, it does so less than our democratic mythologies would have us believe. It also operates to mark and separate the haves from the have nots.

The restructuring of the American economy is changing the costs of a highly stratified organization of work. It is also changing the costs of the dualism within our schools, which is now functioning to lock individuals out of the economic mainstream, either precluding their entry into or making them marginal to the labor market.

A blunt reality that has to be confronted by the privileged is how long they can maintain privilege in a society where the

---

[4]Early reports from work-based apprenticeship demonstrations for youth identify parental resistance as a major barrier. Parents read "apprenticeship" as precluding college and its associated access to higher skill and higher wage jobs.

educational system functions in this way. The costs of not educating all children to the point where their human capital gives them economic opportunity show up in tax burdens and dramatically rising investments in public and private security.

This dualism, manifesting itself in decontextualized academics and academically debased vocational education, is now part of our problem. It blocks a paradigm shift in how we organize learning —a shift that promises to benefit the academically inclined and that is a critical strategy for engaging the less inclined in learning experiences that will develop the skill and knowledge that they need to assume higher-skill and better-paying jobs.

Organize the learning situation around the practices reflected in cognitive apprenticeships

Whatever we want to call it—cognitive apprenticeship, integrating academic and vocational education, constructivist learning, or some other term—we are talking about a different pedagogical paradigm. It is important to see these ideas not as an unintegrated list of learning principles, but as a coherent image of what effective learning situations look like. It is a way of teaching that embodies much of what we understand about how the human being learns.

Let us be absolutely clear about how we see cognitive apprenticeship. It is a paradigm of instruction for all students. It is not a clever renaming of vocational education. It is for the B.A.-bound and the non-B.A.-bound; it is for the brilliant, innovative student destined for one of the country's great universities, the solid student, and the at-risk student. It is for elementary, middle, and high school students. It is for your child and those of your friends, not just for someone else's children. It is not for everything that has to be learned, but it is for much that should be learned, and where it fits what has to be learned, it is for all students.

The analyses of chapters 3 and 4 yield several reasons for recommending a shift to the learning principles of cognitive apprenticeship.

It promises to be a more effective learning strategy for all students, whether motivated or unmotivated. Very simply, it works with, rather than against, the natural learning system of human beings—the desire to make sense out of, interact with, explore, and build control and mastery over the environment.

- For those more committed to school and learning, cognitive apprenticeships promise deeper and more disciplined learning that is better remembered and more appropriately used. The problem with today's organization of learning for this group is not motivational. It is the inefficient and ineffective use of the student's learning time.

- For the less motivated, cognitive apprenticeships promise engagement in the learning process. Observational evidence suggests that learning situations which reflect cognitive apprenticeship principles are highly motivating. This characteristic is important for all students, but especially for those who do not see the point of school or themselves as its customers. We suspect that one difference between those that we separate into the academically more versus less inclined is a difference in the two groups' willingness to tolerate a learning situation that is not particularly efficient, effective, or intrinsically motivating for anyone.

Cognitive apprenticeship structures learning in ways consistent with the knowledge and skills needed in restructured workplaces. Earlier we argued that schools are still best organized to fuel a mass production economy and that the reorganization of work is destroying the fit between traditionally organized work and education. Mapping the learning principles of cognitive apprenticeships against the emerging skill and knowledge requirements of the restructured workplace shows a better match between the two. For example:

- The model stresses not only domain-specific content, but also the cognitive strategies (such as heuristic strategies, cognitive management strategies, learning strategies) required to operate effectively with this content. Thus it emphasizes the cognitive skills that employers in restructured workplaces need in all employees, including those on the shop floor.

- Teachers in cognitive apprenticeships facilitate and guide student learning, but fade as rapidly as possible to give students control over their own learning. This strategy mirrors the relationship between supervisors and the supervised in restructured workplaces.

- The learning environment of cognitive apprenticeships deliberately reproduces the technological, social, chronological, and motivational characteristics of the real-world situations in which what is being learned will be used. Thus, cooperative learning groups mirror the teams of restructured workplaces. Contextualizing what is being learned in ways that reflect the nature of real-world tasks helps students understand the meaning and appropriate use of knowledge and skill in nonschool situations.

Cognitive apprenticeship integrates the dual principles of mind and matter, the theoretical and applied. It represents an image of what bridging the divide between head and hand looks like. Its principles systematically preserve and integrate the best of what today we call academic and vocational education into a single model that can be used to teach mathematics or interior design. Under cognitive apprenticeship, the sole remaining difference between academic and vocational education lies in one element: the domain-specific content of what is being taught.

The best vocational education is more apt to use some of the methods (such as modeling, coaching, or scaffolding and fading) and sociology (such as contextualized and cooperative learning) of cognitive apprenticeship than good academic education. However, even when vocational education picks up pedagogic elements of cognitive apprenticeship, it is generally weak on the content side—in academic knowledge and the higher-order cognitive skills such as heuristic strategies, cognitive management strategies, and learning strategies. Thus cognitive apprenticeship can function as the grounded curricular and pedagogic model for integrating the best of academic and vocational education—as the model for what to teach and for how to teach it.

Cognitive apprenticeship retains the option of postsecondary education for all students. Cognitive apprenticeship is designed to create a well-prepared mind at ease with the demands of real-world tasks and equipped to continue learning. Thus for both teachers and parents it eliminates the historic K-12 conflict between workplace preparation and preparation for postsecondary education.

Cognitive apprenticeship is potentially generalizable to many learning situations. Its learning principles seem appropriate for learners of different ages who have different learning objectives —initial preparation, second chance learning, and retraining as experienced workers. Evidence on this issue is now fragmentary and often anecdotal. However, we do not see any theoretical reasons for limited generalizability.

WHAT DO OUR RECOMMENDATIONS IMPLY FOR THE EDUCATION REFORM DEBATE?

Our analyses of the skill implications of changes in the U.S. economy and of a century of thought and research on learning have led us to three fundamental recommendations:

- change the mission of K-12 schools to position all students for middle- and high-skill jobs

- dissolve the dualism between academic and vocational that perpetuates the deep division between education and the economic preparation of all students

- organize the learning situation around the practices reflected in cognitive apprenticeships

If these ideas are accepted, at least provisionally, they have certain implications for educational reform arguments now on the table, such as *America 2000* (1991) or the U.S. Secretary of Labor's Commission on Achieving Necessary Skills (SCANS, 1991, 1992). Our interest is less in these specific proposals than in the issues that they reflect. Proposals come and go; the problems that generate them are more permanent.

The current reform discussion focuses on content and needs to expand to issues of pedagogy

The current reform discussion focuses on content, but the analysis in this book underscores critical problems with pedagogy that have at least as much to do with college or workplace performance problems as content. The reform discussion needs to be extended to issues of pedagogy.

America 2000 identifies five content areas for K-12: science, mathematics, English, geography, and history. Although these five areas are currently under siege, especially from the arts and foreign languages, the battle is still being waged over content. Pedagogy has not surfaced as a major issue. However, our reading of the research record is that *how* content is taught makes all the difference in whether content is learned, retained, and appropriately used. If we are looking for spectacular improvements in learning, they lie, not solely, but importantly, in pedagogic changes.

Professionally based standards of best practice are needed

In an effort to focus on the point of education—the development of students' skills and knowledge, the reform effort is replacing educational input and process performance measures with outcome standards. The theory, based on some evidence, is that teachers and schools teach to the test. Thus, it is argued, if we get our performance measures right, we will get the skill and knowledge outcomes that we want.

The potential problem with this theory is that it is based on data about teacher and school responses to what have been relatively minor changes in test content, in the operations that students were asked to perform on content, and in the testing context or format. Current discussions of national tests entertain substantial changes in content, in the operations that students are expected to perform on content, and in the assessment method —for example, portfolios or projects rather than multiple-choice tests.

The knowledge and skill needed by teachers to meet these changed standards are not widely distributed throughout the educational system.[5]   We believe that we need professionally based standards of best content and best pedagogic practice to complement outcome standards.   These standards must be professional and substantive, not bureaucratic or regulatory. Standards in this sense are emerging from some disciplinary groups, such as the National Council of Teachers of Mathematics and the National Science Teachers Association.   Some states, such as California and Vermont, have taken curricular design actions that, although originating with government, are professional in nature.

Implementing standards of best practice requires a systematic diffusion strategy and more and better-used resources for teacher retraining

A systematic diffusion strategy. Educational reform debates swing between two "theories" of change. At their extremes, one, often called a "top down" approach, lays down rules or standards "from above" (often from government),[6] sometimes with punitive

---

[5]For example, if the nation decides to include the SCANS competencies in K-12 outcome responsibilities, even the experts are not clear about the pedagogic and curricular mechanisms needed to generate these competencies.

[6]An example of this theory of change is the 1970s federal legislation called "packaging and dissemination." The idea was to develop or identify a good model and then to distribute it widely. The image was somewhat that of putting the model in a box and mailing it, with the expectation that the addressee would open the box, take out its contents, and plug it into the wall. Studies showed that practices do not diffuse within the educational system in this way. Not only did the "addressee" need to understand the practices through working with them in some guided way, but those practices had to be adapted to the particular circumstances of the host institution if they were to be incorporated. This same strategy is implicit in *America 2000*; practices developed in the 535+ schools presumably will diffuse to other schools through a process like packaging and dissemination.

overtones. ("Do it or else.") The other extreme, often called a "bottom up" strategy, argues for letting local practitioners figure things out for themselves, revealing a sometimes excessive faith in local innovation.

The key to successful implementation is not either-or, but both. For example: the principles of cognitive apprenticeship have substantive content grounded in decades of thought and research. Local practitioners are not apt to re-invent these principles either effectively or efficiently, and these principles therefore constitute "external" or "top down" standards.

At the same time, implementation research shows that all principles have to be adapted to their situations of use to be incorporated into practice. Their *intent* needs to be preserved, and whether or not their intent has been preserved in the particular situation needs to be substantiated. However, objectives or intent can be met in various ways in the local situation.

An intriguing strategy for diffusing and incorporating educational innovations may lie in the new corporate practice of "benchmarking" (Camp, 1989; Tucker, Zivan, & Camp, 1987; Caudron, 1991; Altany, 1991), a strategy adopted and extensively developed by the Xerox Corporation. Benchmarking is described by benchmarking experts as a discovery process and a learning experience. It forces constant testing of internal actions against external standards of industry practices. Xerox defines it as "The continuous process of measuring our products, services, and business practices against the toughest competitors or those companies recognized as industry leaders" (Camp, 1989, p. 10).

Benchmarks may be descriptive, as in the description of a best industry practice, or they may be converted to a performance metric which shows the effect of incorporating the practice. The challenge is to close the gap between the current practice and the benchmark.

Although its objectives are similar, benchmarking differs fundamentally and in several ways from conventional diffusion practices in education. First, benchmarking requires the borrower to be much more self-analytic. Which functions within the organization should be benchmarked? Answering this question requires an analysis of the functional organization of the borrower and decisions about which functions, if improved, would most heavily impact attaining the organization's goals. How is the selected function organized? What are key metrics that reveal its performance?

Second, benchmarking is inherently a *comparative* process, the borrower's practices being compared with those that are best-in-class, *wherever those might be found.* The fundamental question is how the borrower's practices stack up against those of organizations identified as having highly productive practices. Although educators normally look to other schools for practices to borrow, benchmarking encourages looking both within and beyond the industry for best-in-class. Thus, Convex Computer visited Disney World to learn about facilities management (Altany, 1991). Xerox selected L.L. Bean as best-in-class in the warehousing and materials-handling function, even though L.L. Bean is in the mail-order retail clothing industry. It looked to Federal Express for billing efficiency and to Cummins Engine for production scheduling. Corning Glass, which has a manufacturing unit designed to meet customers' emergency needs, visited best-in-class hospital emergency wards to understand how to organize teams for crisis work.

Third, the knowledge "borrowed" from best-in-class instances is complex. It includes

- images of what the best practices look like, which can be used as an "organizer" for changes in the borrowing organization

- how these practices perform on the appropriate metrics. If these practices outperform the borrower's, the performance levels they attain become the initial performance target—or benchmark—for the borrowing organization

- guides for how to change practices in the borrower's organization to close the performance gap between the borrower and the benchmark.

Fourth, benchmarking forces borrowers to disaggregate their borrowing to the level of comparable functions. In education we tend to borrow whole programs—this is the logic behind the National Diffusion Network, for example. However, benchmarkers point out that something as complex as a program has numerous functions and subfunctions. No one organization will conduct all program functions at best-in-class levels. The practices that need to be brought together to create a "program" should be assembled from best-in-class instances wherever they exist.

Finally, the concept of benchmarking bridges the gap between two divisive theories of change in education described earlier. Benchmarking is efficient in that it is based on a search for best-in-class practices. However, it is a search, not imposed, but conducted by local practitioners. Benchmarking is also explicit that borrowed ideas must be adapted to the circumstances of the borrower.

More and better-used resources for teacher retraining. Educational reform talk is about changed curricula, new pedagogies, more powerful use of multimedia, computer-based technologies, new ways of assessing student progress, and market-based rewards and punishments for success and failure. Implicit in this talk is a "physician, heal thyself" mentality. But how are teachers supposed to learn and be able to use the objectives, concepts, and methods of new curricula and pedagogy—in some cases, involving computer software programs? *America 2000* barely mentions the teacher retraining that would be required to achieve the curricular and other changes sought by that document.

Ironically, restructuring companies have understood (though often underestimated) the need to retrain their employees not just to handle change, but to fuel it (Wiggenhorn, 1990). We are talking about changes in K-12 schools comparable to those in American companies. The educational system currently carries on retraining activities, but with some notable exceptions, these are often badly designed. We are not making the best use of the retraining resources already available. Retraining curricula and pedagogy are often poorly designed for effective learning. And the retraining of teachers is often not coordinated with the structural changes in the schools that are necessary if teachers are to use their newly acquired skills.

These problems aside, retraining takes teacher time. Realistically, the retraining that educational reforms imply cannot be done in the one or two days that many teachers get during the school year for retraining. This means not just better uses of old money, but new money.

The rethinking of educational assessment now occurring could be consistent with the assessment requirements of cognitive apprenticeship

Cognitive apprenticeship principles imply certain educational outcomes, such as a command of domain-specific concepts, facts, and procedures; a facility with the cognitive strategies required to operate effectively with and on domain-specific knowledge; the ability to initiate one's own learning; or the ability to use the tools and resources critical to performance in nonschool settings.

These outcomes imply the need for the kinds of assessments now being discussed in some (not all) reform circles. The role of multiple-choice tests seems limited to an assessment of facts. These tests do not seem well-designed to assess most of the other outcomes of interest. Written assessments potentially have a much broader role, but even well-designed ones will not be adequate by themselves. Means such as portfolios and projects seem better suited to assess the outcomes of cognitive apprenticeships.

K-12 student performance standards should reflect the standards required in middle- and high-skill jobs

Several national panels and councils[7] are engaged in setting outcome standards for the K-12 system and for individual students. The names, membership, and missions of these panels and councils will change over time. However, wherever we have standard-setting processes, the question arises whether these standards reflect the nature and levels of the skills and knowledge needed for middle- and high-skill jobs. Answering this question requires identifying the skills and knowledge needed in middle- and higher-skill jobs for which K-12 should be held accountable.[8]

Several classes of knowledge and skills are now on the K-12 reform table.[9] *America 2000* identifies five core subjects: mathe-

---

[7]These include the National Council on Educational Standards and Testing, the National Goals Panel, the New Standards Project, and certain subject matter groups, such as the National Council of Teachers of Mathematics.

[8]Since most of these jobs will require post-K-12 training, the K-12 responsibility is to insure that high school graduates exit with the types and levels of skills and knowledge needed to complete the additional training, whether in postsecondary programs or employer-sponsored training.

[9]Corporate-specific skills, such as those required by a company's customized management information system, are not considered the province of K-12 education, although they may be developed at public expense through

matics, science, English, history, and geography. These subjects do not seem to have been selected for their relationship to workplace performance standards. This does not mean that they do not have a relationship; they do. However, *America 2000* makes no argument to this effect; the nature of the relationship is not explored; their sufficiency as preparation for middle- and higher-skill jobs is not addressed; and the levels needed are not specified.

SCANS (1991, 1992) explicitly focuses on the generic skills that are required in a wide range of occupations and industries. The 1991 report talks about foundation or "tool" skills, such as reading, writing, mathematics, listening, speaking, and thinking and problem-solving skills. It also names generic workplace competencies in such areas as managing resources—for example, time or money; interpersonal relationships—for example, performing effectively in teams; managing information; understanding and operating with systems; and handling technology. The foundation skills are seen as instrumental to, but not the same as, the SCANS workplace competencies.

Although SCANS struggled with the question of required performance levels for foundation skills and generic workplace competencies, these skills have not been benchmarked against the workplace to determine the levels needed for middle and higher-skill jobs or for training in these jobs.

The nation needs a technically and politically credible source of information about the foundation and generic workplace skills required across occupations and industries, the levels of these skills that are required, changes in these skills as best workplace practice changes, and the extent to which possession of these skills in fact predict better workplace performance.

---

postsecondary customized training programs.

At the turn of the century Nicolas Murray Butler and Charles Eliot, the presidents of Columbia and Harvard Universities, helped to create what is now known as the College Board. Their objective was to simplify, systematize, and communicate colleges' skill requirements for college entry to high school students and K-12 educators. (Another objective was to improve the quality of secondary education.) We now seem to need analogously visible and organized information about the skills required for workplace entry and for jobs that require middle and high skills.[10]

An analogue to the College Board could help to make employers visible and organized customers of the schools, just as the College Board helped to make colleges visible and organized customers of K-12 education.[11] Colleges have been the primary customer of K-12 education, not employers. In other words, K-12 students and educators customarily organize their activities around postsecondary education. We are consequently in a situation where the K-12 system is stunningly ill-equipped and undisposed to understand the skill implications of the economy as these affect all students, both the B.A.-bound and those whom, traditionally, they have only "carried."

A third and last set of skills for which K-12 has some limited responsibility are occupation- and industry-specific skills, such as programming machine tools, operating radiographic equipment, or analyzing financial data for financial planning purposes. The U.S. Congress and U.S. Departments of Labor and Education are already talking about industry- and occupation-specific boards for

---

[10]We credit Michael Kane with originally suggesting an employer analogue to the College Board.

[11]The U.S. House of Representatives is now considering establishing a National Board on Workforce Skills that would focus on the types and levels of foundation and generic workplace skills needed for workplace entry.

establishing standards and performance levels for this category of skills. Should the U.S. Congress also establish a workplace analogue to the College Board, the nation would have a system of boards in place that span workplace skills from the generic to the occupation- and industry-specific.

WHERE SHOULD APPRENTICESHIPS BE LOCATED: THE WORKPLACE, THE SCHOOL, OR SOME MIXED ARRANGEMENT?

The current explosion of interest in apprenticeship in the United States has conceived of it as work-based, not school-based, for several reasons. The German (and Austrian and Swiss) work-based apprenticeship system is better-known in the United States than the school-based systems of Sweden, Denmark, or France. The U.S. Department of Labor saw the traditional, work-based, apprenticeship programs under its jurisdiction as a platform for a work-based system that could be extended to younger ages and a wider range of occupations. It was also generally acknowledged that many school-based programs—even many vocational ones —are divorced from the needs of the workplace, the disconnect including both the knowledge and skills needed at work and the ways in which knowledge and skills are used in the workplace.

Thus, a work-based system seemed a good solution. It seemed to eliminate the problem of coordinating work-oriented schooling with the workplace because learning and the workplace were coincident with one another. It seemed to reduce the school-to-work transition problem for youth for the same reason.

Work-based apprenticeship presumes (1) an apprenticeship learning situation, and (2) the workplace as the locus of that situation. These are two separate assumptions; one does not logically require the other. The previous section argued for apprenticeship forms of learning, albeit modified to reflect the greater cognitive and theoretical demands of contemporary activities, especially in restructured workplaces. Still unresolved is the optimal location for cognitively oriented apprenticeship. Although we associate apprenticeship with the workplace, it is a paradigm of learning that can be implemented in schools, workplaces, or some combination of school and work.

We can evaluate alternative locations on several criteria. (1) Is the interest in apprenticeship learning broad enough to support a national system? (2) Is the option organized to deliver effective learning? (3) Is it organized to deliver efficient learning? (4) Does it reflect the knowledge demands of the workplace and the work contexts in which knowledge and skill have to be used? (5) Does it develop broadly applicable knowledge and skills? (6) Does it blur the division between the academic and vocational educational tracks?

Is the interest in apprenticeship learning broad enough to support a national system? Neither workplaces nor schools look broadly responsive to apprenticeships, but for different reasons. For employers the issue is their willingness to undertake coherent training of the less educated and the very inexperienced. Although these patterns could change, employers now tend to focus their formal training on the better educated and on the not-so-young (Tan, 1989). Thus, employers' training policies, staffing, and arrangements are structured for an older and better educated group than we envision for work-based apprenticeship. The fact that co-operative learning, a cousin of work-based apprenticeship, has remained a minor work-based educational alternative in the United States is consistent with these traditional investment patterns.

Employers' traditional training patterns reflect structural arrangements that isolated policy incentives cannot be expected to change. When companies shift from mass to flexible organizations of work, we see attendant shifts in their training patterns to include all workers. However, companies make these shifts in response to economic incentives far more powerful than any policies can be expected to generate.

The United States also differs from our competitor nations, such as Germany or Japan, in the social contracts between employers, workers, the educational system, and government. For example, American individualism seems to show up in a tenuous commitment of management and workers to one another, giving employers the flexibility to fire and employees the flexibility to change jobs. Relative to competitor nations, American policy is fairly mute with regard to employers' freedom to fire, layoff, and contract work out. This cross-national policy difference manifests itself in various ways. For example, during recessions the data show that American companies tend to maintain stock dividends and fire workers; Japanese and European employers tend to reduce dividends and retain workers (Lichtenberg, 1992). The relatively tenuous ties between American workers and employers affect the incentives of both parties to invest in skills. Another national difference is how various social benefits, such as health care, are financed. Allocating the costs of health insurance to employers in the United States can further weaken employer-worker ties, in that it creates an incentive for employers to resort to contract workers that are ineligible for company benefits.

Although schools focus on the education of the young and inexperienced, the problem here is their receptiveness to apprenticeship forms of learning. Even a casual comparison of the traditional K-12 paradigm of learning with that of cognitive apprenticeship shows the major changes that will be required to replace one with the other. For example, curricula need to change; teachers' roles shift markedly, requiring retraining; evaluations need to include performance-based assessments, such as portfolios; and the daily schedule needs to change to create the blocks of time required for students to work on problems of significant scope and complexity.

Is the location organized to deliver effective learning? Work-based apprenticeship has tended to assume that if school-based programs are bad learning places for work, workplaces must be good places. This may turn out to be true empirically under some circumstances, but it is faulty logic. In fact, observations of informal on-the-job training of the less educated also raise questions about the workplace as learning place. They show that informal on-the-job training can be catch-as-catch-can. Its quality depends heavily on who happens to be around to train. In work groups with high turnover, almost-novices are training novices, a situation that violates all models of good apprenticeship training. (This problem is analogous to "out of field" teaching in schools, as when the coach is drafted to teach chemistry.) Even experienced members of a group can only pass on their understanding of the job and the corporate context in which this is embedded. This understanding is rarely monitored and can vary wildly (Scribner & Sachs, 1990).

At the same time, another Scribner and Sachs study (1991) shows that the key issue for the workplace as a learning place is the same as for school-based learning. How work or school activities are set up is what enhances or inhibits learning. For example, a company that organizes work or a school that organizes learning as a set of segmented tasks will limit what its workers or its students learn. (Companies with mass production organizations of work will be more apt to structure learning as segmented tasks.) Whether in the workplace or the schoolroom, what is emphasized and encouraged in the setting helps learners develop either a conceptual understanding or a highly routinized, inflexible set of responses. Since most companies follow a mass production organization of work, we may face a Hobson's choice between two worlds (schools and the workplace), neither of which is routinely well designed for powerful learning.

The inherent power of the location to motivate the learner also affects learning effectiveness. Collins, Brown, and Newman (1989) note the motivating quality of a work-based option.

> ...apprentices are encouraged to quickly learn skills that are useful and therefore meaningful within the social context of the workplace. Moreover, apprentices have natural opportunities to realize the value, in concrete economic terms, of their developing skill: well-executed tasks result in saleable products (Collins, Brown, & Newman, 1989, p. 459).

At the same time, actual school-based trials of cognitive apprenticeships show that intrinsically motivating learning situations can be set up in the school (Schoenfeld, 1988; the Vermont example). A motivational key seems to be whether the learning situation is organized around the natural learning system of human beings —around the fact that we are naturally sense-making, problem-solving, and environmentally interactive.

Is the option organized to develop skills and knowledge efficiently? Here the school-based option may have an edge over the work-based option. Collins, Brown, and Newman (1989) point out that the problems and tasks given to learners in standard, work-based apprenticeships arise not from pedagogical, but from workplace, concerns.

> Cognitive apprenticeship selects tasks and problems that illustrate the power of certain techniques, to give students practice in applying these methods in diverse settings, and

> to increase the complexity of tasks slowly so that compo-
> nent skills and models can be integrated. Tasks are
> sequenced to reflect the changing demands of learning.
> Letting job demands select the tasks for students to
> practice is one of the great inefficiencies of traditional
> apprenticeship (Collins, Brown, & Newman, 1989,
> p. 459).

Since a highly motivating work-based apprenticeship means that
individuals learn whatever they are trying to learn quickly, the
inefficiency of a work-based option seems to reside, not in the
initial speed with which learning occurs, but in its potential for
learning "holes" and unnecessary repetition.

*Does the option reflect the knowledge demands of the workplace
and the work contexts in which knowledge and skill have to be used?*
A workplace location seems to be a winner here, with two
caveats. First, if a work-based apprenticeship system picks up a
normal sample of workplaces, it will include many with traditionally organized work contexts. If one objective is to prepare
individuals for a restructuring economy, the nature of the work
contexts has to be monitored carefully.

Second, a key principle of cognitive apprenticeships—which
were developed as school-based—is that they mirror the nonschool conditions under which knowledge and skill are used.
Thus, a school-based option can meet this criterion, but not as
easily as the work-based option.

*Does the option develop knowledge and skills that are broadly
applicable?* We noted earlier that modern activity is relatively
changeable and nonroutine, requiring an arrangement of learning
that develops higher-order cognitive skills and an understanding
of the principles that govern the domain under study. A school-
based option would seem to have the edge here. A work-based
option can be set up to develop higher-order cognitive skills in the

context of the domain being learned. However, the embedded-ness of the learning within a work situation makes it harder to insure that learners grapple with issues and problems outside of the limits of that situation.

At the same time, a work-based option can be designed to develop broader skill and knowledge. Without extensive academic, professional, or even on-the-job training, people can achieve conceptual understanding on the job. Again, the issue is the nature of the individual's job responsibilities—how the work situation is set up. Some work activities, in and of themselves, are educationally rich. The question is the probability of finding such arrangements in the workplace versus the school.

Does the location blur the division between academic and vocational? For reasons described earlier, we think it is critical to blur the distinction between academic and vocational education. In the absence of a national system organized around preparing students for middle/higher-skill jobs, anything other than the academic track and college amounts to no preparation, which at best translates into low-skill jobs.

Also, as we said earlier, parents resist any reform that sounds as though it might preclude college for their children. In fact, early returns from the work-based apprenticeship demonstrations show that parents are reluctant to place their children in work-based apprenticeships. They see these options as foreclosing college for their children, whether or not they in fact do. A school-based cognitive apprenticeship, even if focused on an occupational domain such as interior design, blurs the division better.

In sum, on these six criteria, work-based apprenticeships and school-based cognitive apprenticeships have pluses and minuses. We suspect that some mixed strategy may ultimately turn out to be optimal, but what that strategy might look like is now unclear.

We need much more experience with and analysis of work-based and school-based apprenticeships.

There is a final reason to think carefully about the location of apprenticeship learning. A fundamental impetus for work-based apprenticeships is that schools generally have done a poor job of preparing the non-baccalaureate-bound. The question is whether we should allow schools to avoid taking educational responsibility for this large group of students. If the workplace turns out to be the learning place of choice for this group, well and good. However, we need to be careful that we do not resort to work-based apprenticeships to finesse problems with the schools. We are already paying for second-chance programs and remedial college programs to get done what the K-12 system should have gotten done in the first place.

Increasing firm-based training: When will it help?

We have emphasized two parallel developments—changes in the nature of work and a new understanding of effective learning. What do these imply for employer-sponsored training? Chapter 2 made a simple point: more rapid changes in products and productive processes increase the retraining needs of the adult labor force. Adults may return to school on their own to increase their skills, but under conditions of fairly continuous economic change this ad hoc retraining strategy serves employers' interests poorly. They need systematic policies that finance and arrange for the retraining that their workers need.

Differences between U.S. and foreign competitor companies in amounts of employer-sponsored training has made employer-provided training a controversial public policy issue. The MIT Commission on Industrial Productivity in *Made in America: Regaining the Competitive Edge* (Dertouzos, Lester, & Solow, 1989), the Office of Technology Assessment *Worker Training: Competing in the New Economy* (1990), and the Commission on the Skills of the American Workforce in *America's Choice* (1990) all point to deficiencies in firm-based training as a key problem for U.S. competitiveness. These groups argue that U.S. employers provide less training than their competitors in Japan and in many European countries. The most commonly proposed policy solutions involve either incentives (often tax incentives) for employer-sponsored training or a required minimum training expenditure. A minimum expenditure provision is usually modeled after the French system, which requires that firms spend at least two percent of their payroll expenditures on training. Firms that fall below that figure must pay the difference into a national training fund.

We agree that encouraging employer-based training is important. Currently, the large bulk of employer-provided training goes to higher-level employees such as executives, managers, professionals, and sales workers. As companies change their organization of work, training needs to be extended to all levels of the work force. But current proposals to provide incentives for employer-sponsored training are not likely to have a strong effect on the overall operation of firms or of the economy in general.

First, any effect of training will be blunted without changes in related labor-market institutions. Higher labor turnover in the U.S. makes U.S. employers reluctant to invest in training because they lose this investment if trained workers leave. However, with or without incentives to train, the U.S. turnover problem will probably continue, partly because American government policy and standard business practice favor employment flexibility over job security. In Japan and some European countries, labor market institutions and employment laws make it more difficult for firms to fire or lay off employees. Thus if employers want to strengthen their workforce, they must, more than U.S. employers, invest in incumbent workers. The weakening of unions in the U.S. also probably promotes higher turnover. However, whatever the turnover effects, the decline of unions removes one way in which employees can participate in and bargain over changes in production processes and the role of training in those changes. Proposals to encourage training never call for a more fundamental policy that would address these institutional issues.

Second, earnings analysis suggests that, in general, schooling and training on the job are complementary (Mincer, 1989). Thus the educational system itself provides a crucial foundation for employer-sponsored training, and the effects of employer-sponsored training are reduced without simultaneous reforms of schooling.

Third, relative to physical investments, there are no tax-based disincentives to training whose removal might encourage more employer-sponsored training. Training already receives favorable tax treatment. Although capital equipment must be depreciated over several years, training investments can be written off as current expenditures. Thus any additional incentive to encourage employer-sponsored training will have to come from direct budgetary outlays in the form of tax credits or direct subsidies.

Fourth, training must be connected to new economic opportunities to yield productivity and economic growth payoffs. These new economic opportunities may be new technologies, a reorganization of work within the company, new markets, or new products. Training helps realize the economic potential of innovations, but it is unlikely to have economic impact in the absence of innovations. The basic challenge lies in creating these opportunities.

Fifth, policy discussions about the need for increases in firm-based training have virtually ignored questions about the nature and quality of employer-sponsored training. The content and quality of education that workers receive on the job are related to the organization of work. What we have characterized as ineffective learning in schools, such as passive learning, also shows up in corporate learning situations. Since this form of learning generally fits traditionally organized workplaces, it is only challenged when workplaces restructure. In other words, the conflict between traditionally organized work and more effective models of learning is deeper than the fact that traditional production processes do not require higher skills. Effective learning clashes directly with the basic foundation of the traditionally organized workplace. As a result, without significant work reform, incentives to encourage employer-sponsored training will tend to expand ineffective approaches to learning.

Two fundamental implications emerge from this discussion. First, we need to understand much more about the nature of teaching and learning on the job. Even basic data on employer-sponsored training are partial and often flawed (e.g., Bartel, 1989). Second, the reform of production processes and of employer-sponsored training are inextricably linked. Indeed, the most powerful reform strategy for corporate training is probably one that eliminates the separation between job training and production, a separation now firmly grounded in traditional approaches to both learning and work.

CONCLUSION

We suggest that our economic and educational institutions face virtually the same challenge. That challenge is to organize their activities, whether learning or production, to capture the power of the fact that human beings are naturally sense-making, problem-solving, and environmentally interactive. This means that our educators and employers have to reconceptualize human potential, thought, and action.

REFERENCES

Alper, W., Pfau, B.N., & Sirota, D. (1985). *The 1985 national survey of employee attitudes.* New York: Business Week and Sirota and Alper Associates.

Altany, D. (1991). Share and share. *Industry Week.* July 15, pp. 12-17.

America 2000: An education strategy. (1991). Washington, DC: U.S. Department of Education.

American Apparel Manufacturers Association (AAMA). (1989). *Making the revolution work: How to implement flexible manufacturing through people.* Washington, DC: Technical Advisory Committee of the Association.

A nation at risk. (1983). Washington, DC: National Commission on Excellence in Education.

Bailey, T. (1988). *Education and the transformation of markets and technology in the textile industry.* New York: Institute on Education and the Economy, Teachers College, Columbia University.

_____. (1989). *Technology, skills, and education in the apparel industry.* New York: Institute on Education and the Economy, Teachers College, Columbia University.

_____. (1991, March). Jobs of the future and the education they will require. *Educational Researcher, 20,* 11-20.

Bartel, A.P. (1989). *Utilizing corporate survey data to study investments in employee training and development.* New York:

Institute on Education and the Economy, Teachers College, Columbia University.

Bartel, A., & Lichtenberg, F. (1987, February). The comparative advantage of educated workers in implementing new technology. *Review of Economics and Statistics, 69* (1), 1-11.

Bertrand, O., & Noyelle, T. (1988). *Human resources and corporate strategy: Technological change in banks and insurance companies of five OECD countries.* Paris: Organization for Economic Cooperation and Development.

Bransford, J.D., Stein, B.S., Arbitman-Smith, R., & Vye, N.J. (1985). Three approaches to improving thinking and learning skills. In J.W. Segal, S.F. Chipman, & R. Glaser (Eds.), *Thinking and learning skills: Relating instruction to basic research* (pp. 133-200). Vol. 1. Hillsdale, NJ: Erlbaum.

Brown, J.S., Collins, A., & Duguid, P. (1989, January-February). Situated cognition and the culture of learning. *Educational Researcher, 18* (1), 32-42.

Callahan, R.E. (1962). *Education and the cult of efficiency.* Chicago: University of Chicago Press.

Camp, R.C. (1989). *Benchmarking. The search for industry best practices that lead to superior performance.* Milwaukee, WI: ASQC Quality Press.

Carraher, T.N., Carraher, D.W., & Schliemann, A.D. (1985). Mathematics in the streets and in schools. *British Journal of Developmental Psychology, 3,* 21-29.

Caudron, S. (1991, April). How Xerox won the Baldridge. *Personnel Journal*, 98-102.

Clark, K., Chew, B., & Fujimoto, T. (1987). Product development in the world auto industry. *Brookings Papers on Economic Activity, 3*, 729-71.

Collins, A., Brown, J.S., & Holum, A. (1991, Winter). Cognitive apprenticeship: Making thinking visible. *American Educator*, 6-11, 38-46.

Collins, A., Brown, J.S., & Newman, S. (1989). Cognitive apprenticeship: Teaching the craft of reading, writing, and mathematics. In L.B. Resnick (Ed.), *Knowing, learning and instruction: Essays in honor of Robert Glaser* (pp. 453-494). Hillsdale, NJ: Erlbaum.

Commission on the skills of the American workforce. (1990). *America's choice: High skills or low wages!* Rochester, NY.: National Center on Education and the Economy.

Cremin, L.A. (1961). *The transformation of the school*. New York: Knopf.

Dertouzos, M., Lester, R., & Solow, R. (1989). *Made in America: Regaining the competitive edge*. Cambridge, MA: MIT Press.

Dewey, J., & Dewey, E. (1915). *Schools of tomorrow*. New York: Dutton.

DeWitt, K. (1991, April 24). Vermont gauges learning by what's in portfolio. *The New York Times*, p. A23.

diSessa, A.A. (1982). Unlearning Aristotelian physics: A study of knowledge-based learning. *Cognitive Science, 6,* 37-75.

_____. (1983). Phenomenology and the evolution of intuition. In D. Gentner & A. Stevens (Eds.), *Mental Models* (pp. 15-33). Hillsdale, NJ: Erlbaum.

Eaton, A.E., & Voos, P.B. (1991). Unions and contemporary innovations in work organization, compensation, and employee participation. In L. Mishel & P.B. Voos (Eds.), *Unions and Economic Competitiveness* (pp. 173-215). Armonk, NY: M.E. Sharpe.

Farnham-Diggory, S. (1990). *Schooling.* Cambridge: Harvard University Press.

The forgotten half: Pathways to success for America's youth and young families. (1988). Washington, DC: Final Report, Youth and America's future: The William T. Grant Foundation Commission on Work, Family, and Citizenship.

Gallup, A.M. (1985, September). The 17th annual Gallup Poll of the public's attitudes toward the public schools. *Phi Delta Kappan, 67* (1), 35.

Harding, P. (1988). The strategic role of technological innovation in the textile industry. Speech presented at the International Forum sponsored by the Antonio Ratti Foundation on "The Textile Sector and the New Technological Era: What Prospects?" Como, Italy.

Hass, M. (n.d.) *Cognition-in-context: The social nature of the transformation of mathematical knowledge in a third-grade classroom*. Irvine, CA: University of California, Social Relations Graduate Program.

Hayes, J.R., & Simon, H.A. (1977). Psychological differences among problem isomorphs. In N.J. Castellan, Jr., D.B. Pisone, & G.R. Potts (Eds.), *Cognitive Theory* (pp. 21-41). Hillsdale, NJ: Erlbaum.

Herndon, J. (1971). *How to survive in your native land.* New York: Simon and Schuster.

Higuchi, Y. (1987). A comparative study of Japanese plants operating in the U.S. and American plants: Recruitment, training, wage structure, and job separation. Discussion Paper No. 8. New York: Columbia University Center on the Japanese Economy and Business.

Hill, P., Foster, G.E., & Gendler, T. (1990). *High schools with character*. R-3944-RC. Santa Monica, CA: The RAND Corporation.

Holyoak, K.J. (1985). The pragmatics of analogical transfer. In G.H. Bower (Ed.), *The psychology of learning and motivation,* 19 (pp. 59-87). New York: Academic Press.

Ichniowski, C., Lewin, D., & Delaney, J. (1988). *The new human resource management at the workplace.* Paper presented at the First Regional Congress of the Americas, International Industrial Relations Association, Quebec City.

Jordan, B. (1987). *Modes of teaching and learning: Questions raised by the training of traditional birth attendants.* Report No. IRL87-0004. Palo Alto, CA: Institute for Research on Learning.

Katz, H. (1985). *Shifting gears: Changing labor relations in the U.S. automobile industry.* Cambridge, MA: MIT Press.

Kochan, T., Cutcher-Gershenfeld, J., & MacDuffie, J.P. (1989). *Employee participation, work redesign and new technology: Implications for public policy in the 1990s.* Paper prepared for the U.S. Department of Labor, Commission on Workforce Quality and Efficiency.

Lave, J. (1988a). *Cognition in Practice.* Cambridge: Cambridge University Press.

_____. (1988b). *The culture of acquisition and the practice of understanding.* Report No. IRL88-0007. Palo Alto: Institute for Research on Learning.

_____. (in press). *Tailored learning: Education and everyday practice among craftsmen in West Africa.*

Lave, J., Smith, S., & Butler, M. (1988). Problem solving as an everyday practice. In *Learning Mathematical Problem Solving.* Report No. IRL88-0006. Palo Alto: Institute for Research on Learning.

Lehman, D.R., Lempert, R.O., & Nisbett, R.E. (1988). The effects of graduate training on reasoning: Formal discipline and thinking about everyday life events. *American Psychologist,* 43 (6), 431-442.

Levin, H. (1987). Improving productivity through education and technology. In G. Burke & R. Rumberger (Eds.). *The future impact of technology on work and education* (pp. 194-214). New York: The Falmer Press.

Levin, J.A. (1982). Microcomputers as interactive communication media: An interactive text interpreter. *The Quarterly Newsletter of the Laboratory of Comparative Human Cognition,* 4, (2), 34-36.

Levy, F., & Murnane, R. (in press). U.S. earnings levels and earnings inequality: A review of recent trends and proposed explanations. *Journal of Economic Literature.*

Lichtenberg, F.R. (1992, February 16). In a downturn, cut profits before jobs. *New York Times,* Section 3, p. 13.

Marchese, J. (1991, August 11). A shop rat's tale. *The New York Times Magazine,* pp. 31-32, 58-ff.

Martin, L.M.W., Scribner, S., & Beach, K. (1990). *Learning to use computerized machinery on the job.* Paper presented at the Annual Meeting of the American Educational Research Association.

Mincer, J. (1989). *Labor market effects of human capital and of its adjustment to technological change.* Unpublished conference paper. New York: Institute on Education and the Economy, Teachers College, Columbia University.

Mincer, J., & Higuchi, Y. (1988). *Wage structures and labor turnover in the U.S. and in Japan.* New York: Institute on Education and the Economy, Teachers College, Columbia University.

Morris, N.M., & Rouse, W.B. (1985). Review and evaluation of empirical research in troubleshooting. *Human Factors, 27* (5), 503-530.

National Council on Vocational Education. (1990). *"Time for Action"*: *A business, industry, and education forum.* Washington, DC: National Council on Vocational Education.

Nisbett, R.E., Fong, G.T., Lehman, D.R., & Cheng, P.W. (1987). Teaching reasoning. *Science, 238,* 625-631.

New York Stock Exchange. (1982). *People and productivity: A challenge to corporate America.* New York: New York Stock Exchange.

Office of Technology Assessment (OTA). (1987). *The U.S. textile and apparel industry: A revolution in progress.* Washington, DC: U.S. Government Printing Office.

_____. (1988). *Technology and the American economic transition: Choices for the future.* OTA-TET-283. Washington, DC: U.S. Government Printing Office.

_____. (1990). *Worker training: Competing in the new economy.* OTA-ITE-457. Washington, DC: U.S. Government Printing Office.

Palincsar, A.S., & Brown, A.L. (1984). Reciprocal teaching of comprehension-fostering and monitoring activities. *Cognition and Instruction, 1,* 117-175.

_____. (1989). *Knowing, learning, and instruction: Essays in honor of Robert Glaser.* Hillsdale, NJ: Erlbaum.

Pea, R.D. (1989). *Socializing the knowledge transfer problem.* Report No. IRL89-0009. Palo Alto, CA: Institute for Research on Learning.

Pechman, E.M. (1990). *The child as meaning maker: The organizing theme for professional practice schools.* Unpublished paper commissioned by the American Federation of Teachers.

Perkins, D.N., & Salomon, G. (1989, January-February). Are cognitive skills context-bound? *Educational Researcher, 18* (1), 16-25.

Pressley, M., Snyder, B.L., & Cariglia-Bull, T. (1987). How can good strategy use be taught to children? In S.M. Cormier & J.D. Hagman (Eds.), *Transfer of Learning* (pp. 81-120). New York: Academic Press.

Raizen, S.A. (1989). *Reforming education for work: A cognitive science perspective.* Berkeley, CA: National Center for Research in Vocational Education.

Resnick, L. (1986). Constructing knowledge in school. In L.S. Liben & D.H. Feldman (Eds.), *Development and Learning: Conflict or Congruence* (pp. 19-50). Hillsdale, NJ: Erlbaum.

_____. (1987, December). Learning in school and out. *Educational Researcher, 16,* 13-20.

Salomon, G. (1990). Studying the flute and the orchestra: Controlled experimentation vs. whole classroom research on computers. Unpublished paper. Tucson, AZ: University of Arizona.

SCANS (See U.S. Secretary of Labor.)

Scardamalia, M., & Bereiter, C. (1985). Fostering the development of self-regulation in children's knowledge processing. In S.F. Chipman, J.W. Segal, & R. Glaser (Eds.), *Thinking and*

Learning Skills: Research and Open Questions, (pp. 563-577). Hillsdale, NJ: Erlbaum.

Schoenfeld, A.H. (1985). *Mathematical problem solving.* New York: Academic Press.

_____. (1988). *Ideas in the air.* Report No. IRL88-0011. Palo Alto, CA: Institute for Research on Learning.

Schultz, C. (1975, September). The value of the ability to deal with disequilibria. *Journal of Economic Literature, 13,* 827-46.

Scribner, S. (1988). *Head and hand: An action approach to thinking.* New York: Institute on Education and the Economy, Teachers College, Columbia University.

Scribner, S., & Fahrmeir, E. (1982). *Practical and theoretical arithmetic: Some preliminary findings.* Working Paper No. 3. New York: City University of New York, Graduate Center, Industrial Literacy Project.

Scribner, S., & Sachs, P. (1990). *A study of on-the-job training.* New York: Institute on Education and the Economy, Teachers College, Columbia University.

_____. (1991). *Knowledge acquisition at work.* New York: Institute on Education and the Economy, Teachers College, Columbia University.

Shanker, A. (1990, July 8). Here we stand. *The New York Times,* p. E7.

Silvestri, G.T., & Lukasiewicz, J.M. (1991, November). Occupational employment projections. *Monthly Labor Review, 114* (1), 64-94.

Singley, M.K., & Anderson, J.R. (1989). *The transfer of cognitive skill.* Cambridge, MA: Harvard University Press.

Spenner, K. (1983). Deciphering Prometheus: Temporal change in the skill level of work. *American Sociological Review, 48,* 824-73.

_____. (1985). Upgrading and downgrading of occupations. *Review of Educational Research, 55,* 125-154.

Stalk, G. (1988, July-August). Time—The next source of competitive advantage. *Harvard Business Review, 88* (4), 44-51.

Stanback, T. (1990). The changing face of retailing. In T. Noyelle (Ed.), *Skills, wages and productivity in the service sector.* Boulder, CO: Westview Press.

Stasz, C., McArthur, D., Lewis, M., & Ramsey, K. (1990). *Teaching and learning generic skills for the workplace.* R-4004-NCRVE/UCB. Berkeley, CA: National Center for Research in Vocational Education.

Stevenson, H.W. (Author). (1989). *The polished stones.* [Film]. Ann Arbor, MI: Center for Human Growth and Development, University of Michigan.

Stevenson, H.W., & Stigler, J.W. (1992). *The learning gap.* New York: Summit Books.

Sticht, T. (1989). Adult literacy education. In E.Z. Rothkopf (Ed.), *Review of Research in Education, 1988-89, 15.* Washington, DC: American Educational Research Association.

Stigler, J.W., & Stevenson, H.W. (1991, Spring). How Asian teachers polish each lesson to perfection. *American Educator,* 12-20, 43-47.

Stillings, N.A., Feinstein, M.H., Garfield, J.L., Rissland, E.L., Rosenbaum, D.A., Weisler, S.E., & Baker-Ward, L. (1987). *Cognitive science: An introduction.* Cambridge: MIT Press.

Tan, H. (1989). *Private sector training in the United States: Who gets it and why.* New York: Institute on Education and the Economy, Teachers College, Columbia University.

Taylor, F.W. (1911). *The principles of scientific management.* New York: Harper.

Thomas, R., & Kochan, T. (1990). *Technology, industrial relations, and the problem of organizational transformation.* Paper prepared for the Conference on Technology and the Future of Work, Stanford University.

Thorndike, E.L. (1898). *Animal Intelligence.* New York: MacMillan.

Tucker, F.G., Zivan, S.M., & Camp, R.C. (1987, January-February). How to measure yourself against the best. *Harvard Business Review, 87* (1), 2-4.

U.S. Department of Commerce, Bureau of the Census. (1991). *Statistical abstract of the United States: 1991.* Washington, DC.

U.S. Secretary of Labor's Commission on Achieving Necessary Skills (SCANS). (1991). *What work requires of schools.* Washington, DC: U.S. Department of Labor.

_____. (SCANS). (1992). *Learning a living: A blueprint to high performance.* Washington, DC: U.S. Department of Labor.

Vaughan, R.J., & Berryman, S.E. (1989). *Employer-sponsored training: Current status, future possibilities.* New York: Institute on Education and the Economy, Teachers College, Columbia University.

Voos, P. (1987, January). Managerial perceptions of the economic impact of labor relations programs. *Industrial and Labor Relations Review, 40,* 195-208.

White, B.Y. (1983). Sources of difficulty in understanding Newtonian dynamics. *Cognitive Science, 7,* 41-65.

_____. (1984). Designing computer games to help physics students understand Newton's laws of motion. *Cognition and Instruction, 1,* 69-108.

Whyte, W.H. (1956). *The organization man.* New York: Simon and Schuster.

Wiggenhorn, W. (1990, July-August). Motorola U: When training becomes an education. *Harvard Business Review, 68* (4), 71-83.

Womack, J.P., Jones, D.D., & Roos, D. (1990). *The machine that changed the world.* New York: Macmillan Publishing Company.

RELATED PUBLICATIONS

The ideas presented in this book are grounded in extensive research in several areas. Readers are invited to explore the research and related policy analyses in the following publications of the Institute on Education and the Economy.

1. CHANGES IN THE NATURE AND STRUCTURE OF WORK

Bailey, T. December, 1989. *Changes in the Nature and Structure of Work: Implications for Skill Requirements and Skill Formation.* (64pp.) $7.50.

_____. October, 1989. *Technology, Skills, and Education in the Apparel Industry.* (57pp.) $7.50.

_____. April, 1988. *Education and the Transformation of Markets and Technology in the Textile Industry.* (42pp.) $7.50.

Bailey, T. and T. Noyelle. April, 1988. *New Technology and Skill Formation: Issues and Hypotheses.* (19pp.) $7.50.

Noyelle, T. November, 1990. *Skill Needs and Skill Formation in Business Services: The Case of the Accounting, Management Consulting, and Computer Software Industries.* (48pp.) $7.50.

_____. April, 1988. *Services and the New Economy: Toward a New Labor Market Segmentation.* (11pp.) $3.50.

2. EDUCATION, TRAINING,
AND ECONOMIC OUTCOMES

Altonji, J. July, 1990. *Controlling for Personal Characteristics, School and Community Characteristics, and High School Curriculum in Estimating the Return to Education.* (22pp.) $7.50.

_____. February, 1990. *Accounting for Uncertain Outcomes in Estimating the Return to Education.* (11pp.) $7.50.

_____. September, 1990. *The Effects of High School Curriculum on Education and Labor Market Outcomes.* (66pp.) $7.50.

_____. November, 1990. *The Demand for and Return to Education When Education Outcomes are Uncertain.* (42pp.) $7.50.

Bartel, A.P. and F. Lichtenberg. October, 1989. *The Age of Technology and Its Impact on Employee Wages.* (19pp.) $7.50.

Kett, J.F. December, 1989. *From Useful Knowledge to Vocational Education, 1860-1930.* (42pp.) $7.50.

Mincer, J. February, 1991. *Human Capital, Technology, and the Wage Structure: What Do Time Series Show?* (37pp.) $7.50.

_____. February, 1990. *Education and Unemployment of Women.* (29pp.) $7.50.

_____. November, 1989. *Human Capital Responses to Technological Change in the Labor Market.* (23pp.) $7.50.

_____. October, 1989. *Education and Unemployment.* (34pp.) $7.50.

_____. February, 1989. *Labor Market Effects of Human Capital and of Its Adjustment to Technological Change.* (53pp.) $7.50.

Mincer, J. and Y. Higuchi. June, 1988. *Wage Structures and Labor Turnover in the U.S. and in Japan.* (52pp.) $3.50.

Sicherman, N. October, 1989. *Education and Occupational Mobility.* (19pp.) $7.50.

_____. April, 1989. *"Over-Education" in the Labor Market.* (27pp.) $7.50.

Vaughan, R.J. December, 1989. *Education, Training, and Labor Markets: Summary and Policy Implications of Recent Research by Jacob Mincer.* (29pp.) $7.50.

Vinovskis, M. December, 1989. *The Role of Education in the Economic Transformation of the Nineteenth Century.* (32pp.) $7.50.

3. EMPLOYER-SPONSORED TRAINING

Altonji, J. and J.R. Spletzer. November, 1990. *Worker Characteristics, Job Characteristics, and the Receipt of On-the-Job Training.* (37pp.) $7.50.

Bailey, T. February, 1989. *Changes in the Nature and Structure of Work: Implications for Employer-Sponsored Training.* (22pp.) $7.50.

Bartel, A.P. February, 1989. *Utilizing Corporate Survey Data to Study Investments in Employee Training and Development.* (21pp.) $7.50.

Mincer, J. November, 1990. *Job Training, Wage Growth, and Labor Turnover.* (37pp.) $7.50.

_____. July, 1990. *Job Training: Costs, Returns, and Wage Profiles.* (22pp.) $7.50.

Noyelle, T. February, 1989. *Skills, Skill Formation, Productivity and Competitiveness: A Cross-National Comparison of Banks and Insurance Carriers in Five Advanced Economies.* (16pp.) $7.50.

Tan, H., B. Chapman, C. Peterson, and A. Booth. *Youth Training in the United States, Britain, and Australia.* (47pp.) (Document No. R-4022-ED) Santa Monica, CA: The RAND Corporation, 1991. (To order this document, please contact The RAND Corporation Publication Department at 1700 Main Street, P.O. Box 2138, Santa Monica, CA, 90406-2138.)

Tan, H. February, 1989. *Private Sector Training in the United States: Who Gets It and Why?* (55pp.) $7.50.

Vaughan, R.J. February, 1989. *Public Subsidies and Private Training.* (23pp.) $7.50.

Vaughan, R.J. and S.E. Berryman. February, 1989. *Employer-Sponsored Training: Current Status, Future Possibilities.* Synthesis of findings from papers prepared for the Conference on Employer-Sponsored Training. (35pp.) $7.50.

4. LEARNING IN AND FOR THE WORKPLACE

Scribner, S. and J. Stevens. April, 1989. *Experimental Studies on the Relationship of School Math and Work Math.* (54pp.) $7.50.

Scribner, S. and P. Sachs. July, 1990. *A Study of On-the-Job Training.* (96pp.) $7.50.

Scribner, S. and P. Sachs. February, 1991. *Knowledge Acquisition at Work.* (78pp.) $7.50.

5. REFORMING EDUCATION: A COGNITIVE SCIENCE APPROACH

Berryman, S.E. September, 1991. *Cognitive Science: Challenging Schools to Design Effective Learning Environments.* (54pp.) $7.50.

_____. December, 1989. *Portents of Revolution: The Cognitive Sciences and Workplace Literacy.* (7pp.) $3.50.

Raizen, S. October, 1989. *Reforming Education for Work: A Cognitive Science Approach.* (84pp.) (To order this document, please call the National Center for Research in Vocational Education Publication Department at 800-637-7652.)

Scribner, S. April, 1988. *Head and Hand: An Action Approach to Thinking.* (17pp.) $3.50.

6. EDUCATION AND TRAINING POLICY

Berryman, S.E. July, 1990. *Skills, Schools, and Signals.* (20pp.) $7.50.

_____. May, 1990. *When American Businesses Change: The Imperatives for Skill Formation.* (9pp.) $3.50.

_____. January, 1990. *What Do We Need to Teach? To Whom? When? How?* (35pp.) $7.50.

_____. January, 1989. *Education and the Economy: A Diagnostic Review and Implications for the Federal Role.* (45pp.) $7.50.

_____. July, 1987. *Breaking Out of the Circle: Rethinking Our Assumptions About Education and the Economy.* (9pp.) $3.50.

_____. March, 1987. *Shadows in the Wings: The Next Educational Reform.* (10pp.) $3.50.

Briefings Given at the Conference on Education and the Economy: Hard Questions, Hard Answers. September, 1989. (59pp.) $10.00.

Crain, R.L., A.L. Heebner, and Y. Si. *The Effectiveness of New York City's Career Magnet Schools: An Evaluation of Ninth Grade Performance Using an Experimental Design.* April, 1992. (109pp.) (Document No. MDS-173) Berkeley, CA: National Center for Research in Vocational Education. (To order this document, please call the National Center for Research in Vocational Education Publication Department at 800-637-7692).

Education and the Economy: Hard Questions, Hard Answers. September, 1989. Executive Summaries of Conference Background Papers. (91pp.) $10.00.

Glennan, T.K. September, 1989. *Education, Employment, and the Economy: An Examination of Work-Related Education in Greater Pittsburgh.* (43pp.) (Document No. N-3007-OERI/HHE. To order this document, please contact The RAND Corporation Publication Department at 1700 Main Street, P.O. Box 2138, Santa Monica, CA, 90406-2138.)

Hoachlander, E.G., P. Kaufman, and E. Wilen. August, 1990. *Indicators of Education and the Economy.* (56pp.) $7.50.

McDonnell, L.M. December, 1989. *Restructuring American Schools: The Promise and the Pitfalls.* (59pp.) $7.50.

Natriello, G. April, 1989. *What do Employers Want in Entry-Level Workers? An Assessment of the Evidence.* (13pp.) $3.50.

Vaughan, R.J. December, 1989. *Mixing Metaphors: Education and Economic Development Policy.* (47pp.) $7.50.

In addition to the above research reports and policy analyses, the Institute on Education and the Economy publishes nontechnical information Briefs for a general audience.   There is no charge for the Briefs.

Altonji, J. November, 1990. *The Decision to Start College: Factoring in the Uncertainty.* (2pp.)

Bailey, T. January, 1990. *The Changing Occupational Structure.* (4pp.)

Bailey, T. and T. Noyelle. April, 1989. *The Impact of New Technology on Skills and Skill Formation in the Banking and Textile Industries.* (4pp.)

Bartel, A.P., F.J. Lichtenberg, and R.J. Vaughan. November, 1989. *Technological Change, Trade, and the Need for Educated Employees: Implications for Economic Policy.* (4pp.)

Berryman, S.E. September, 1991. *Designing Effective Learning Environments: Cognitive Apprenticeship Models.* (4pp.)

Crain, R.L., A.L. Heebner, and Y. Si. June, 1992. *The Effectiveness of New York City's Career Magnet Schools.* (4pp.)

Glennan, T. November, 1990. *Community-Based Strategies for Work-Related Education.* (4pp.)

McDonnell, L.M. November, 1989. *Restructuring American Schools: The Promise and the Pitfalls.* (4pp.)

Natriello, G. April, 1989. *Do We Know What Employers Want in Entry-Level Workers?* (4pp.)

Natriello, G., A. Pallas, and E. McDill. March, 1992. *Post-High School Employment and Schooling Patterns of Non-College Bound Youth.* (4pp.)

Scribner, S. and P. Sachs. December, 1991. *Knowledge Acquisition at Work.* (4pp.)

——————. August, 1990. *On the Job Training: A Case Study.* (4pp.)

Tan, H. November, 1990. *Youth Training in the U.S., Great Britain, and Australia.* (4pp.)

Vaughan, R.J. August, 1990. *Education, Training, and Labor Markets: A Policy Perspective.* (4pp.)

Vaughan, R.J., and S.E. Berryman. November, 1989. *Employer-Sponsored Training: Current Status, Future Possibilities.* (4pp.)

Except where otherwise noted, all publications in this list are available from the Institute on Education and the Economy, Teachers College Box 174, Columbia University, New York, NY 10027. (212-678-3091)